M000158506

"This broad-ranging book gives much practical advice for living conscientiously in today's world."

—Judith Sutera, OSB
Mount St. Scholastica, Atchison, Kansas

SAINT BENEDICT FOR BOOMERS

Wisdom for the Next Stage of Life

Christine M. Fletcher

LITURGICAL PRESS
Collegeville, Minnesota

www.litpress.org

Quotations from the Rule of St. Benedict are taken from *Rule of Saint Benedict 1980*. Edited by Timothy Fry. Collegeville, MN: Liturgical Press, 1981. Used with permission.

Scripture texts in this work are taken from the *New Revised Standard Version Bible: Catholic Edition* © 1989, 1993, Division of Christian Education of the National Council of the Churches of Christ in the United States of America. Used by permission. All rights reserved.

Excerpts from the English translation of the *Catechism of the Catholic Church* for use in the United States of America copyright © 1994, United States Catholic Conference, Inc.—Libreria Editrice Vaticana. English translation of the *Catechism of the Catholic Church: Modifications from the Editio Typica* copyright © 1997, United States Catholic Conference, Inc.—Libreria Editrice Vaticana. Used with Permission.

© 2017 by Order of Saint Benedict, Collegeville, Minnesota. All rights reserved. No part of this book may be reproduced in any form, by print, microfilm, microfiche, mechanical recording, photocopying, translation, or by any other means, known or yet unknown, for any purpose except brief quotations in reviews, without the previous written permission of Liturgical Press, Saint John's Abbey, PO Box 7500, Collegeville, Minnesota 56321-7500. Printed in the United States of America.

1   2   3   4   5   6   7   8   9

Library of Congress Cataloging-in-Publication Data

Names: Fletcher, Christine M., author.
Title: Saint Benedict for boomers : wisdom for the next stage of life / by Christine M. Fletcher.
Description: Collegeville, Minnesota : Liturgical Press, 2017. | Includes bibliographical references.
Identifiers: LCCN 2016041518 (print) | LCCN 2016048869 (ebook) | ISBN 9780814647028 | ISBN 9780814647271 (ebook)
Subjects: LCSH: Older people—Religious life. | Aging—Religious aspects--Christianity. | Benedict, Saint, Abbot of Monte Cassino.
Classification: LCC BV4580 .F56 2017 (print) | LCC BV4580 (ebook) | DDC 248.8/4—dc23
LC record available at https://lccn.loc.gov/2016041518

To that great cloud of witnesses,
especially Helen and Claude Moerder, my parents,
who showed me how to live and how to die

Contents

Preface   ix

Chapter 1   Why Benedict?   1

Chapter 2   Long Life   12

Chapter 3   Eat Less but Eat Right   29

Chapter 4   Purpose after Work   55

Chapter 5   Witness of Life   75

Chapter 6   Accepting Our Cross,
            Hoping in the Resurrection   94

Chapter 7   The Art of Dying   113

Notes   129

Preface

"Don't trust anyone over 30!" If you are a boomer like me, you remember uttering that phrase and really meaning it. Yet here we are moving in our 50s and 60s and probably looking at another 20 years of life. What are we going to do with those years? How are we going to serve God and our neighbor now as we face big life changes, retirement, health challenges, and the loss of our friends and family members? I would like to make some suggestions based on my own family circumstances, my study of theology, and the Rule of St. Benedict.

I grew up in a very funny family (in many ways), but one of the strangest things about us is how spread out the generations are. I was born 20 years after my brothers and sisters; I was born an aunt with a niece and a nephew 2 and 3 years older than me. I have a photo of my parents' 25th wedding anniversary with their grown children, and I am not yet even a gleam in Dad's eye. My father was born in 1896, 12 years after his brothers and sisters, the son of my grandfather's second wife. My grandfather was born in 1856. We have 3 generations spanning 158 years; demographers usually consider 25 years a generation. Growing up in this spread-out family, I saw all stages of life. This age spread gave a richness to our big family that was one of the joys of my childhood. I learned to care for children while babysitting my sisters' children; I saw my parents, sisters, and brothers age and die. Now I have had to attend their funerals, one after another, following cancer, and strokes, and other diseases. My parents had a healthier old age than my siblings. My parents had hard physical work throughout their life; my siblings lived a life of relative ease.

At one point, I read about St. Dominic on his deathbed saying that he had perhaps been more pleased to talk to young women than to old.[1] I read this when I was 35, halfway to the 70 years the Bible promises us. For the first time I felt old and realized that I had to prepare for aging, not just let it creep up on me.

When my children were leaving home for university, I found myself crying over their baby pictures and wondering what in the world I was going to do now. My life had been centered on the family, taking part-time work, but seeing my primary job as that of wife and mother. Now no one seemed to need my mothering. At that time I was living in Britain, actually fourteen miles from Cambridge. I realized I could fulfill a dream and do a PhD, something that would not have been possible in the United States, with four children to put through university. But there I had the option. My husband encouraged me, even though he warned that I probably wouldn't find a job, because of age discrimination. The examiners for my PhD agreed, saying that I shouldn't waste time and money applying for jobs in Britain, but that it was worth trying for jobs in the US.

As it happened, I was hired by Benedictine University, and my husband and I started a new stage of our life and marriage. He retired from his medical practice and became the househusband; I became a professor of theology. It was a healthy switch for both of us, although it took us a while to adjust to each other in our new roles. He likes being in charge of his schedule (mostly) and being able to put his time into volunteer work, reading, and computer programming. Although he does a superb job of preparing healthy meals for us, he would never say he loves cooking. I love having the structure of a full-time job, with colleagues, an office of my own, and challenging work. We feel very blessed, especially as my work means we are living near St. Procopius Abbey, where we attend the liturgy and participate in the monks' daily prayer. From our garden we can hear the abbey bells. We became Benedictine oblates.

The new job gave me a new lease on life. I felt young, especially being surrounded by college students, and constantly having to learn new things. So it comes as an unwelcome surprise to look in the mirror and see my mother's aging face look back at me. Mentally I feel 45; physically I am 66. Health problems took me by surprise; I was diagnosed with cancer at 63. At about the same time, my nephew (55) was diagnosed with a melanoma. He called me when he heard about my diagnosis and we agreed that having cancer meant that for the first time we realized that the phrase "we're all going to die" applied to us. We weren't getting a pass. Our experience brought us face-to-face with our mortality, like Hezekiah, who pleaded with the Lord for more time to set his house in order (Isa 38). We both were very lucky; the cancer was found very early, and treated promptly and successfully, but the experience still reminds me that I do not know what the day will bring. Saint Benedict tells us to remind ourselves that we are going to die every day (RB 4.47).[2] Now is the time to make things right.

So, this book. It is based on the idea that no one can retire from being a Christian; we are to love God and our neighbor throughout our life. And it recognizes that aging presents us with change, loss, and death, as well as new growth and opportunities for deep gladness and peace. I am not trying to minimize the challenges and difficulties, but to see how we can redeem them in this life as we prepare for the next. All change is also loss, even change that we want and strive for, and all loss must be mourned. We must face the changes in our life with courage and call upon the Holy Spirit for the wisdom to live this stage of our life as witnesses to God's love and mercy.

Our faith gives us a purpose in life: to love God and to love our neighbor as ourselves. This, the Great Commandment (Matt 22:36-40; Mark 12:28-31), gives us a guide to life that is valid when we are healthy and strong and when we are weak and sick. We still have much to contribute to life and those around us, even when we are ill and dependent. Our faith makes us part of a larger community that supports us when we are ill and alone. We, on our part, can pray and offer our suffering for the good of others. There is a tradition in Catholicism that the dying have duties to God and to the living. Death must be faced with courage because for the Christian death is not the end but the beginning. As the funeral liturgy says, "Life is changed not ended."

One of the wisest guides to life is St. Benedict of Nursia. His Rule has been guiding people who seek God for fifteen hundred years. His wisdom is perennial, and is helpful to us today as we negotiate new challenges in living well, preserving our bodily health, discerning our purpose in this new stage of living, deepening our faith, and facing sickness and death.

A new stage of life can be a time of deeper conversion to our identity as God's beloved children. So the book starts with St. Benedict, and how his Rule can help anyone grow in faith and relationship with Christ. The chapter on St. Benedict, his Rule, and Benedictine spirituality offers a guide to deepening our prayer life and seeing our life not as split between sacred and secular, but as a unified whole. This integration of faith and life is the work of a lifetime, and this stage of our life offers us challenges such as sickness as well as opportunities such as new free time. Saint Benedict can guide us as we strive to make the love of God and neighbor real in our new stage of life, every day, wherever we may be—even on the golf course, "[f]irst and foremost, there must be no word or sign of the evil of grumbling" (RB 34.6).

The next two chapters deal with the practicalities of living and aging, looking at recent work on longevity and health. Maintaining our health is part of loving ourselves, as God wants us to. Chapter 2 looks at antiaging versus longevity research and then at physical activity as necessary for healthy aging. Chapter 3 puts advice on a healthy diet into a theological framework of gratitude and Eucharist. In these chapters and throughout the book I will be challenging our culture's assumption that the individual is supreme and can make any choice. As Catholic Christians, we know that to be a person means to be in relationship. We bear the image of God, and the God we worship is a Trinity: God's very being is relationship. So throughout this book we examine these ideas of pursuing good health and put them into the Christian and Benedictine concept of community and the common good. We will always be looking not just at whether our individual choices are moral, but also at how our individual actions affect the community around us.

The book then moves onto having a purpose, a community, and a vibrant faith at this stage of our life. Chapter 4 looks at purpose after our paid work ends. In America our work often defines us; we introduce ourselves with our occupation. Retiring brings a sudden loss of status and, even though it may be welcomed, it necessarily brings us a big change that must be mourned, before we begin a new phase of life. We can be a resource for the church, bringing the faith to a new generation and taking up new roles of service to our neighbor. We then turn to chapter 5, which discusses how we can be witnesses to Jesus, people who bring the good news of God's love for us to others through our daily life and choices. Our model for this is Jesus' hidden life in Nazareth.

In the final section of the book we look at sickness, suffering, and death, which will inevitably come to us and to those we love. Society may say that suffering is pointless; death is feared by everyone. The wisdom in our tradition is that suffering is redemptive—not pointless or meaningless. We know that death is not the end, but too often we treat it like a final exam without asking what passing it means, missing the ultimate happiness God has planned for his children. We have a sure and certain hope of the resurrection, but we must go through our own Good Friday first. In all this we have faith and hope in the love of God, who will never abandon us, but will bring us to the fullness of life and love in the heart of the Trinity itself.

This book would not be possible without a community: my family and friends, the monks and oblates of St. Procopius Abbey, and my colleagues at Benedictine University. I would especially like to thank Peter, my husband, for his support and encouragement; Joy and Paul Fleckser for reading the manuscript and giving me such good advice for improvements; Fr. Robert Barringer, CSB, for his careful reading, proofreading, and theological help; Fr. Gabriel Baltes, OSB, for his insights as a pastor; and Fr. Philip Timko, OSB, for his guidance and suggestions of theological resources. Fr. Becket Franks, OSB, and the attendees at the Days of Reflection that Fr. Becket and I offer at St. Procopius Abbey have been an immense help and encouragement in seeing how relevant the Rule of St. Benedict is to life today. All of these have greatly helped with my writing; the weaknesses and errors that remain are mine.

CHAPTER 1

Why Benedict?

There are many great spiritual writers and traditions of spirituality. Some of us are acquainted with Dominicans or Franciscans or Jesuits and their traditions. These later spiritualities owe much to the Benedictines, whose influence on the church began in the 600s and continues to this day. Saint Benedict is venerated as a saint in the Roman Catholic, Eastern Orthodox, and Anglican churches. Orthodox Christian Olivier Clément writes of Benedictine monasticism that "Benedictine monasteries [are] still today places of the undivided Church."[1] Saint Benedict is venerated as the father of Western monasticism, and is the patron saint of Europe and of students. His appealing personality shines throughout his Rule. To appreciate his wisdom, we will look at his life, and then at his Rule with its principle *Ora et Labora*, pray and work. Benedict's Rule is useful for a modern twenty-first-century retiree because it has perennial wisdom about life: how to live in community, how to balance the demands of daily life and the spiritual life, and how to pray. His Rule can be a practical guide for us to love God, our neighbor, and ourselves as we enter this new stage of life.

Benedict of Nursia

Saint Benedict was a young Roman from a good family who lived from around 480 to 543. He studied in Rome but as a young man was disgusted by the loose living of the students and the general malaise of the city. He left the city to seek God. This sounds like a strange thing to do, so it requires some explanation. In the early days Christianity was a persecuted religion. The Roman government didn't care what gods you worshiped as long as you would make sacrifices to Caesar. Of course the Jews, and then the Christians, wouldn't do this. So they were considered atheists, and from time to time persecuted. As you can imagine, this meant that being a Christian wasn't something to take lightly. It meant a real commitment. The sponsor for a candidate who wanted to become a Christian had to guarantee that this person wasn't a government informer. The community demanded a long period of instruction so that they could observe the life of the converts, and be sure that they understood what they were getting into.

We have the accounts of the early martyrs like St. Polycarp.[2] In the Roman catacombs the martyrs' tombs were sites for Christian worship, and their example of courage for the faith inspired the church. In 313, Emperor Constantine began the process of making Christianity the state religion. Christians were now becoming free to fully participate in society. As everyone knew, the emperor favored the faith (though he put off his own baptism until the last possible moment, keeping a bishop with him at all times to ensure he would be able to be baptized in an emergency); it became more and more fashionable to be a Christian. It no longer required the courage of the early believers and martyrs.

From the earliest days of the church, those who wanted to experience the total dedication to God of the early martyrs withdrew from the cities to the deserts, especially in Egypt and

Palestine, where they built hermitages. The fame of these holy men and women spread, and visitors would come out from the cities to see them and get a word of advice. Saint Antony the Great, one of the most famous hermits, was visited by St. Athanasius, who wrote the *Life of St. Antony*, which we have today. John Cassian did the tour, and wrote up the stories of the people he had met.

In the East, St. Basil of Caesarea founded monasteries, as did St. Pachomius in Egypt and St. Sabas in Palestine, where instead of living as hermits, people who wanted to seek God lived in community. Basil's sermons and writings, including the Rules for his communities, circulated in the literate world. So, when Benedict wanted to seek God above all else, he had a path to follow. He left Rome and eventually lived in a cave in a small town, Subiaco, in the mountains. Romanus, a monk in a neighboring monastery, befriended Benedict, guided and helped him. Benedict grew in grace and holiness. He, like other holy hermits, attracted followers; eventually he founded twelve monasteries at Subiaco, before he moved to Monte Cassino, where he founded another great monastery. For the guidance of his monks, he wrote the document we know today as the Rule of St. Benedict.

The Rule of St. Benedict

At first glance, it may seem unlikely that a document written in the sixth century for people who wanted to leave the world and live a demanding ascetical life in community could have any relevance to a boomer who wants to have a healthy, meaningful retirement. However, the human condition has not changed since Benedict's day; Jesus Christ is the same yesterday, today, and forever. Benedict gave us not a "to-do list" of how to be holy, but wise principles that he expected his followers to adapt to local conditions. We know that Benedictine monks and sisters don't live the Rule according to the letter of the Rule, but according to the spirit of it. Benedict understood the human heart, that unchanging reality. Culture changes— we don't think corporal punishment is such a great spiritual remedy as Benedict's world did—but we still are human beings struggling with pride, disobedience, laziness, greediness, and all the other deadly sins. Benedict understood human beings, and gave practical guidance to those who are "ready to give up your own will, once and for all, and armed with the strong and noble weapons of obedience to do battle for the true King, Christ the Lord" (RB Prol. 3). That description applies to any Christian who prays the Our Father, in which we say, "thy kingdom come, thy will be done." Benedict helps us put what we pray into practice.

Benedict was the master of moderation. He wrote his Rule for beginners who want to seek God. Today communities of men and women known as Benedictines and Cistercians still live according to this Rule. Laypeople, Catholic and Protestant, are attracted to Benedictine spirituality, which is rooted in God's word. Those laypeople who wish to commit to living their lives by the Rule as adapted to their circumstances can become oblates of a Benedictine monastery. Anyone, whether or not one wants to be an oblate or a monk, can benefit from reading Benedict's Rule and using its wisdom.

For people who want to deepen their spiritual life, Benedict is a sure and faithful guide. There are many translations available, and the complete Rule and the daily reading, the chapter from it that Benedictines around the world read every day in their communities, can be found on the internet.[3] All references to the Rule in this book come from the small book *RB 1980: The Rule of St. Benedict in English*, which has chapter and verse divisions and also has the Scripture passages italicized and identified for easy reference.[4] The Rule is designed to help us to heaven, and we get there by prayer and works. Prayer is primary for Benedict so we begin with that.

Benedictine Prayer

"First of all, every time you begin a good work, you must pray to him most earnestly to bring it to perfection" (RB Prol. 4). Benedict saw idleness as the soul's enemy, so every monk had to work every day. But their most important work was prayer, the *Opus Dei*, the work of God. Prayer is how our relationship with God is built and nourished. God is love and loves us all the time. We can live without acknowledging God and his love for us, but that leaves us in darkness. Prayer is opening ourselves to that love, like opening the blinds to a bright sunny day. When we pray, we experience God's love for us as unique people. He has a plan for each of us. Not only does he want all of us to be happy with him forever in heaven, but he has given us our bodies, personalities, talents; and put us in the world in a family, a place, and a time so that we can make a difference. Each of us has a special role in making the world reflect God's kingdom, by building families and communities that are just and welcoming to everyone, including the weak, the stranger, and the outcast. This work is fueled by prayer.

We can pray using our own words to have an extended conversation with God; we can pray by stopping to really look at and appreciate nature or the face of a person. We can pray by using our minds as we study. We can pray by learning to sit in silence to wait for the still, small voice of God. We can pray the Morning Offering, which gives to God everything we do and experience in the day to come. We can pray with a rosary. Pray as you can!

Prayer is the heart of any spirituality, and every spirituality has a pattern of prayer; Benedict's goal is that we pray always, as the Bible tells us we should (Luke 18:1; Eph 6:18; 1 Thess 5:17-18).

Benedictine spirituality is grounded in Scripture, the word of God. There is communal prayer, which includes psalms, hymns, readings from the Bible, and intercessions, and there is private prayer, known as *lectio divina* (holy reading), which is meditation on Scripture. In both forms of prayer, Benedict wants us to engrave the word of God on our hearts, so that God's word becomes the content of our thought and speech. In the RB 1980, the editors have italicized and cited all the Scripture passages so that we can see at a glance how Scripture was Benedict's vocabulary. Look at this passage from the Prologue to the Rule:

> Let us get up then, at long last, for the Scriptures rouse us when they say: *It is high time for us to arise from sleep* (Rom 13:11). Let us open our eyes to the light that comes from God, and our ears to the voice from heaven that every day calls out this charge: *If you hear his voice today, do not harden your hearts* (Ps 94 [95]:8). And again: *You that have ears to hear, listen to what the Spirit says to the churches* (Rev 2:7). And what does he say? *Come and listen to me, sons; I will teach you the fear of the Lord* (Ps 33[34]:12). *Run while you have the light* of life, *that the darkness* of death *may not overtake you* (John 12:35). (RB Prol. 8-13)

The Word has penetrated so deeply into his mind and heart that Benedict thinks and speaks in Scripture. Reading this we experience this loving God with all his heart, soul, and mind (Matt 22:37). This is what Benedict wants for his followers—that they would meet Jesus, the Word of God in Scripture, which is his living presence, and become more like him, to "put on the Lord Jesus Christ" (Rom 13:14) as St. Paul tells us.

The Opus Dei, the Work of God

Benedict had his priorities clear: prayer and work. But prayer comes first. Benedictine monks and sisters call their times of praying together the work of God, *Opus Dei*. This is their commitment to making their relationship with God the most important priority of life. They gather to pray the psalms, sing hymns, hear readings from Scripture, and pray for the world. This is also known as the Divine Office: "Office" because it is an obligation that was undertaken freely. Benedict wanted his followers to pray in common seven times spread throughout the day from sunrise to sunset, and once in the middle of the night; each of these is called an Office and has a name, such as Lauds, Matins, Vespers, and so forth. This practice of interrupting whatever you are doing to go to communal prayer is a way of sanctifying time, and is characteristic of Benedictine spirituality. Private prayer, work, and recreation balance the times of communal prayer.

Benedict wanted to have the formal times of prayer to help keep the focus of the day on God. By praying the psalms, they are praising God in God's own words. The psalms cover every human emotion: awe, joy, sadness, bewilderment, and anger. Benedict uses them all, even the cursing psalms. By saying the psalms over and over—the Rule stipulates that they pray all 150 psalms each and every week—these psalms start to live in the heart, and at moments when you need a phrase, one from the psalms comes to mind. Benedict reminds his followers to remember that they are praying in the presence of God: "let us stand to sing the psalms in such a way that our minds are in harmony with our voices" (RB 19.7). This is the challenge of all prayer. You know you are making progress when you grow in love of your neighbors. But, fair warning! Praying honestly means facing the dark places inside us, the wounds we bear and the sins we commit. It isn't all warm fuzzy feelings; it is real work.

It is easier to pray the Office if you are in a group, and many parishes have public Morning Prayer (Lauds) or Evening Prayer (Vespers). If you are near a monastery, usually their schedule will allow times when the public is invited to join the community for prayer. However, if you are on your own, you can still use these prayers. There are prayer books and apps available that give you the day's Mass texts and Breviary (another name for the Divine Office). The advantage of this prayer is that you are praying with the whole church, and are taken out of yourself. The structure of the Office means you are adoring, praising, and thanking God before getting to the supplications, the "gimmes." I found this really helpful when I was overwhelmed by life, like being at home with young children or sitting with my dying mother. The psalms and readings should be said aloud to help concentration, and to slow us down to really hear God's word. Reading it aloud means we are seeing the words on the page, hearing the words with our ears, and speaking the words with our mouths; the three senses are helping engrave the Word on our hearts.

Lectio Divina

Lectio divina, meaning divine or holy reading, is the Benedictine way of meditating on Scripture privately.[5] *Lectio* is a slow, attentive reading of the Bible, preferably aloud, letting God speak to us through the Scriptures. The "technique" is to read the passage of Scripture, pause and let it sink into us; read it again, pause and listen to God; read it again, pause. Remember this is to engrave the Word on our hearts. We are reading for layers of meaning. The literal sense of the text is the foundation. What do the words mean? When we understand that we can move onto the spiritual meanings of the text. The early Christian fathers of the church saw spiritual meanings in the Bible: first the allegorical, which tells us about Christ, then the moral, which tells us how we should act, and finally the anagogical, which refers to God's overall plan for life and his kingdom.

Lectio divina takes practice. Like all prayer, it requires quieting the inward chatter to tune into God. I find the framework of *lectio*, and the four senses of Scripture, give me something to hold onto when distractions arise. It is good to start by clearing away distractions; if necessary say a quick prayer about them and then let go. One of the gospels, perhaps the Sunday gospel reading, would be a good starting point; or one of the gospels read through from beginning to end in daily prayer. I like a study Bible that has notes that explain unfamiliar words and give context. I especially like the Ancient Christian Commentary on Scripture volumes.[6] In these, a passage is given, followed by selections from the fathers of the church commenting on that passage. This way, I read the passage and then the fathers, which enlighten me as to how they saw the text. Then I go back and begin the *lectio*.

Sometimes a word or phrase will stay with you for days. For example, in Mark 10 Bartimaeus, the blind beggar, is calling out to Jesus to have pity on him. Jesus calls him, "So throwing off his cloak, he sprang up and came to Jesus" (Mark 10:50). That phrase, especially "throwing off his cloak," just resonated with me. I needed to sit with it for days. Even as I write this, I am drawn back into seeing that total commitment to Christ— Bartimaeus has thrown off his cloak, the only thing that protects him from the elements. He discards everything and springs up! No reluctance.

The movement of prayer in *lectio* begins with the word or phrase that attracts our attention as we listen closely to God. I had to use the notes and guides to Scripture to understand the literal meaning, that the cloak was Bartimaeus's total wealth. Then in prayer I look for the allegorical meaning; in this passage the meaning about Christ is clear: it is Christ who will heal us. Then the moral sense: we need to leave everything and come to him and ask him to help us see. Finally the anagogical sense: we shall see, not just this world, but the coming kingdom of God. Don't rush through stages, but sit with the Word as God speaks to your heart.

Does all this happen every time we pray? No, of course not. This passage took me days. We are human beings who have ups and downs, good days and bad. The sustained practice of *lectio divina* will be uncomfortable, as more and more of the hidden places of our hearts are brought into the light. We are meeting Truth, Goodness, and Beauty itself; our shoddy, tawdry sins will look awful in that light. That is the moment we must remember that God has promised us his mercy—all we need to do is ask and have faith.

Putting It into Practice

By now you may be saying, I want to retire, not enter a monastery. Remember, laypeople adapt the Rule to their lives. I maintain that the foundation for a healthy retirement is an active, regular prayer life. Of course, that is true in every stage of life, but when I was looking after four active children, some days it was all I could do to pray for help and thank God at the end of the day that we all survived and were still speaking to one another.

My job brought us to St. Procopius Abbey. My husband and I are able to attend liturgy at the abbey church. We became oblates of the abbey. This has closed the loop for both of us. I was raised an evangelical Protestant, and Peter was an Anglican who spent his youth singing in the choir. We felt immediately at home in the Benedictine spirituality; after all it is "all Bible." Our shared prayer now is to wake up and say Morning Prayer together, attend daily Mass on occasion (some weeks are better than others), and pray the Our Father together before bed. I try to keep up with *lectio*, but have periods when I use other forms of prayer (and some days when little prayer happens).

Morning Prayer means we have started the day praising God, and have brought our petitions to him. This is what works for us, and a wise spiritual director once told me, "Pray as you can, not as you cannot"—in other words, just pray. God understands it all. Remember what St. Paul told us: "Likewise the Spirit helps us in our weakness; for we do not know how to pray as we ought, but that very Spirit intercedes with sighs too deep for words" (Rom 8:26).

Setting a firm foundation on prayer, we can look ahead to how to live in a way that leads to our flourishing physically, emotionally, and spiritually. The next section looks at two aspects of physical health—exercise and diet—and puts these into the framework of faith and wisdom of Benedict.

CHAPTER 2

Long Life

Paradoxes

Being a Christian is always a paradoxical undertaking—we must be focused on eternal life, and yet always involved with this world. We use the image of a crucified man as a sign of new life. We know that earth is not our home, and yet celebrate creation as good. These paradoxes extend into our attitude to aging: we must accept the truth that we are getting old, and we must stay young at heart. Indeed, Matthew tells us that when the disciples asked about greatness, the Lord said, "Truly I tell you, unless you change and become like children, you will never enter the kingdom of heaven. Whoever becomes humble like this child is the greatest in the kingdom of heaven" (Matt 18:3-4).

More central to our spiritual life, we must accept weakness, dependency, and ultimately death, and yet remain cheerfully confident that God's love will be with us every step of this journey. If we took God's promises seriously, that our destiny is to be happy with him forever in the next world, we would understand why St. Thérèse, the Little Flower, when she was a child, would tell her mother and father that she hoped they would die so they could be with Jesus.

Aging is frightening in a culture that does not honor its elders. In twenty-first-century America the young and healthy are valued, and the old are viewed as decrepit, failing, losing their charms and their minds bit by bit. We structure our society to make the old invisible. Tony Hillerman captured our bizarre societal attitudes in his mystery novels set on the Navajo reservation in the Southwest United States. Navajo culture honors its elders and celebrates family; one of the worst insults is to say that someone is acting as if he or she had no family. In one novel the Navaho detective Jim Chee sees a nursing home in Los Angeles surrounded by a chain-link fence:

> Chee strolled along the fence, looking at the five who lined the porch. This was a side of white culture that he'd never seen before. He'd read about it, but it had seemed too unreal to make an impression—this business of penning up the old. The fence was about six feet high, with the top-most foot tilted inward. Hard for an old woman to climb that, Chee thought. Impossible if she was tied in a wheelchair. Los Angeles seemed safe from these particular old people.[1]

This picture of the old being fenced off from life and the community, reduced to being inmates with no freedom, is one of the terrifying realities of growing old, at least for me. The loss of autonomy happens not because nursing home administrators are mean Nurse Ratcheds, but because health and safety risk management standards mean that the residents are no longer allowed to choose how they live their life. No evening drink unless your doctor writes a specific order for it; foods that you like are forbidden because they may raise your blood pressure or your blood sugar. In some ways the "better" the facility, the worse the problem is. Melissa Nussbaum compared two retirement facilities in an article in the *National Catholic Reporter*. In one her mother-in-law is on various medications and is carefully monitored, which means she cannot eat and drink what she likes. Nussbaum writes, "My husband went to see his mother and brought her a sliver of cheesecake. She asked for it, ate it with relish and was scolded later because the blood sugar stick reveals her sin. Her body has become a confessional with an LED scroll running across the outside ledge; anyone can see her transgressions displayed." She compares this to her aunt, who is much poorer and cared for in a small town, but "somehow, in a little town devoid of medical specialties or expertise, the caregivers have learned the secret. My aunt spends her last days as she chooses. She eats when she's hungry and she eats what she wants. She comes and goes as she likes. She sees her friends and family. She may cross over carrying some still-warm caramel corn."[2] I know that's how I want to die—enjoying life even if my blood pressure is high.

Fear of dependency and illness are not just about our wish to be healthy and active; it is about our fear of financial ruin. The medical-industrial complex is geared toward care in institutions; a frightening article in *The New York Times* documented one woman's struggle to fulfill her father's wish that he die in his own home. She was up against the combined bureaucratic weight of the Medicare and Medicaid establishment. Unable to quit her own job to give her father full-time care, in the end he died in an institution, and she is left feeling as if she failed him in his greatest need.[3] No wonder we are seeing movements to make assisted suicide legal.

Obviously as Christians we do not share this view. Care for others no matter how old, sick, or dependent should be and is one of our highest priorities as a church and as individual Christians. But we are affected by living in our culture and absorbing the messages that culture sends us. We need to step back and actively plan how we are going to spend the final years of our life, and how we want to die. As boomers, we have always led trends. The cutting edge of our generation has recognized the challenges we face and so Jane Fonda, Jane Pauley, and Andrew Weil, for example, have written books telling us how to have a healthy old age, how to reinvent ourselves, and how to enjoy this stage of life too. Other books investigate exceptionally long-lived people and their cultures and give us the rules to change our lives. It is a remarkable paradox that we, who live in one of the most technologically advanced societies in the world, are now looking at subsistence farming cultures to gain knowledge about how to live a long, healthy life.

The Battle against Aging

There is a growing antiaging industry supplying cosmetics, supplements, exercise techniques, plastic surgery, and a whole new range of tests, therapies, and medications. Think of the thousands of dollars spent each year on antiwrinkle creams (I write as someone who has four different kinds on my dressing table and wrinkles on my face). Our culture is a visual culture. We are constantly looking at screens. We are surrounded by images of beautiful young men and women, which distorts our perception of beauty. Because an aging face reminds us that we are mortal, we don't want to look at the old. We miss the beauty of every human being, because we make the airbrushed models our picture of perfection.

Antiaging medicine seems designed to help us fend off the appearance of aging. It has been around for a long time. Reportedly, the Clinique La Prairie in Clarens-Montreux attracted many famous clients including Winston Churchill, Dwight Eisenhower, and Pope Pius XII, who had cells from fetal sheep injected into them. Pope Pius was so impressed he admitted the physician who developed this treatment into the Pontifical Academy of Sciences.[4] This sort of therapy is still on offer at that clinic and others in Mexico. Today, doctors in the United States are touting treatments such as injections of human growth hormone. Plastic surgeons have developed laser treatments and Botox injections to supplement their standard face-lifts. All of this is directed at rejuvenation or stopping the clock. However, biogerontologists tell us there is no such thing as antiaging medicine; there is no way to stop the clock or reverse the aging process.[5]

News reports of medical research add to our delusions about aging and disease. How often have you read a story that claims that some new treatment would prevent deaths from cancer? Our ears and brain stop at "prevent death," even though we must know that even if the treatment cured every cancer, those people were going to die from something else. We want the illusion that death is preventable. Most of us are confused by the way health information is presented to us. And we are not alone. Research has found that even doctors are poor interpreters of statistics.[6]

My point is not that health screenings are bad. My criticism is aimed at our desperate search to deny the truth that we are aging and will die. The attitude of the "worried well"—those who have adequate nutrition, good immunization and access to medical care, who seek more and more preventative medicine, and drug therapies for life extension—is helping to create a health system that is ever more costly and yet fails to provide the most basic care to a large number of our citizens, including many children. This is an issue of social justice, and we must recognize our part in it.

Doctors are trained to focus on the patient; this means that all of our interaction with them confirms our thinking that we make our decisions about health care as individuals. We rarely think about the health of our fellow citizens when politicians are debating tax cuts or tax increases, or new legislation to cover health care. Our health care system is so large and so complicated, it is hard to manage our own care and negotiate with insurers and all the care providers. However, all of our health care choices affect others. This is a serious justice issue, especially for Catholics who are called to judge all their actions by the standard of the preferential option for the poor. When we consume health care without a thought or concern for the health of everyone, it is the same as eating without giving a thought to those who do not have enough food. Our priorities are distorted, and we are harming ourselves as well as others. Our reluctance to face the truth about aging and the inevitability of death has high societal costs, which we will look at again in chapter 6.

There is no way to stop the clock or reverse the aging process. This is the truth that we need to accept, and when we do, Scripture tells us, the truth shall set us free. What we can do is work on maintaining good health habits, which we hope will help us avoid common diseases that make aging even more difficult and shorten our life span. If we approach longevity research in this spirit, not denying the reality of aging but trying to age well, we are being good stewards of our bodies and living the command to love ourselves properly.

The Temple of the Holy Spirit

C. S. Lewis describes three common attitudes to the body. The first sees the body as the prison of the soul; the second makes the body the ultimate good; and the third is that which St. Francis expressed by calling his body "Brother Ass." Lewis prefers the third, because it captures our experience of our own bodies, "both pathetically and absurdly beautiful."[7] Saint Paul reminds us that our bodies are temples of the Holy Spirit. When I mentioned this book to a friend, and said I was going to use that quote, he remarked that the last time he had heard that phrase was in high school when Sister wanted them to be sexually pure. Well, yes, it certainly does apply to sexual purity but it means so much more. Paul wrote to the Corinthians, "Do you not know that you are God's temple and that God's Spirit dwells in you?" (1 Cor 3:16), before he went on to his discussion of sexual purity. Later, in the sixth chapter after urging them to avoid all sin, he wrote, "Or do you not know that your body is a temple of the Holy Spirit within you, which you have from God, and that you are not your own? For you were bought with a price; therefore glorify God in your body" (1 Cor 6:19-20).

This importance of the body is affirmed in the Apostles' Creed when we say, "I believe in . . . the resurrection of the body." This should give us a clue that our bodies are really significant. Lewis, in *The Screwtape Letters*, described human bodies as "those vast and perilous estates, pulsating with the energy that made the worlds in which they [human beings] find themselves without their consent and from which they are ejected at the pleasure of Another."[8] Our body is not a container with a soul rattling around inside it; we *are* our bodies. Only the union of the body and the soul constitutes the human being that is in the image of God.[9]

The body is a remarkable thing; the psalmist was right to praise God for the gift of it:

> For it was you who formed my inward parts;
>   you knit me together in my mother's womb.
> I praise you, for I am fearfully and wonderfully made.
>   Wonderful are your works;
> that I know very well.
>   My frame was not hidden from you,
> when I was being made in secret,
>   intricately woven in the depths of the earth.
> Your eyes beheld my unformed substance. (Ps 139:13-16)

It is astonishing to realize that each of us started as a single cell that divided and specialized and grew until we are the adults we have become. The church's teaching that all life is sacred and has dignity, no matter how small (single cell) or old or sick or handicapped, recognizes that God gave us our bodies and so we have a dignity no one can take away. He redeemed our bodies by taking on flesh in Jesus Christ and rising from the dead. Our bodies are destined for a glorious future. Respecting the gift of life in our bodies demands that we take proper care for them here and now. In that spirit let's look at what we can learn from longevity research.

Longevity Research

Longevity research is a growing field, as more and more people seem to be interested in prolonging their healthy lives. One of the first and best studies on longevity was of the School Sisters of Notre Dame, who agreed to help epidemiologists who were interested in studying Alzheimer's disease. The study began in 1986 and is a good example of excellent scientific method: the sisters all live a similar life, eating the same food, living on the same schedule, and doing similar work. In addition, they all wrote autobiographies when they entered the community, which gave the researchers a clue as to their early outlook, language use, and thinking patterns. Finally, many sisters allowed their brains to be studied after their death, allowing the scientists to check for the physical signs of Alzheimer's.

The researchers found that the risk of death in any given year after age sixty-five is about 25 percent lower for the School Sisters of Notre Dame than it is for the general population of women in the United States.[10] The School Sisters were an excellent population to study because records of their births and adult lives were easily accessible. Researchers studied all aspects of their lives, and reported some common features that turn up in later longevity studies. The sisters ate a wide variety of fresh fruits and vegetables; had a positive outlook, a profound faith, and a supportive community. Some of the healthiest and longest lived also were the most physically active throughout their lives and kept walking as long as they could.[11]

These factors—diet, exercise, purpose, faith, and community —are repeated in the new research on communities with a high number of healthy centenarians, the so-called "blue zones" because the first researchers marked the communities in Sardinia with the highest proportion of men over one hundred years old in blue. Subsequent researchers have applied the term to other communities that have an extraordinarily high number of healthy centenarians. Recently scientists are studying populations in Okinawa, Sardinia, and Loma Linda, California (where a lot of Seventh-day Adventists live), among other places with higher than average concentrations of long-lived people. These communities do have accurate birth records, and so are suited for longevity research.

Current research into longevity proposes a set of habits for a healthier lifestyle: move naturally, eat less, eat more plants rather than meat and processed foods, drink red wine in moderation, have a strong sense of purpose, take time to relieve stress, participate in a spiritual community, make family a priority, and be surrounded by those who share these values.[12] These sound like simple recommendations until we look at our society and how disconnected from a healthy lifestyle most of us are.

The Slothful Society

Most of us think of sloth as simply being physically lazy, and that really is a major part of the sin. But it is more than that.

Dorothy L. Sayers described it well: "It is not merely idleness of mind and laziness of body; it is that whole poisoning of the will which, beginning with indifference and an attitude of 'I couldn't care less,' extends to the deliberate refusal of joy and culminates in morbid introspection and despair."[13] This is the kind of sloth we often see in ourselves when we continue in unhealthy habits. We reject doing something about them because it will be a trouble, and we will be uncomfortable. We can slip into a kind of despair. Our mental and physical states are connected. We are our bodies. The mental state of sloth is reflective of a physical state where we are no longer active participants in life, not even by-standers but by-sitters.

There is a second kind of sloth, though, the hyperactive kind; again, Sayers described it well: "It is one of the favourite tricks of this Sin to dissemble itself under cover of a whiffling activity of the body. We think that if we are busily rushing around and doing things, we cannot be suffering from Sloth."[14] Wendy Wasserstein in a humorous book on sloth calls these people the übersloths,

> [who] can spend an hour on a stationary bicycle in a spin class racing at 70 mph to nowhere. It is a metaphor for their lives, which are full of sound and fury, but like the best of sloths, signify nothing. . . . Whether you're a traditional sloth or a New Age übersloth, we are all looking at the possibility of real thought, and rejecting it. Better to fall into line than to question the going ethos, whether it be fashion, family, or even religion. True creativity requires some amount of not just initiative but the courage to fall out of line.[15]

Both busyness and laziness serve as excuses for not exercising our bodies, our minds, and our spirits. Yet to have a healthy old age we need to exercise all three and recognize how interconnected they are.

Move Naturally

Our society has invented more and more labor-saving devices. I rejoice in them especially for the freedom they have brought to women. When I was growing up, I had to help do the wash with an old-fashioned wringer washer because my mother thought doing the sheets and towels might break the new automatic washer her children had gotten her. That experience gave me a real respect for women of previous generations who faced a family wash *day* with hours of physical labor. We had to fill the wash tubs and washer with water carried in buckets, then put in the clothes, put them through the wringer, manually move them in the rinse water, put them through the wringer, manually rinse them again, put them through the wringer, and finally take them either outside on a sunny day or up three flights of stairs to the attic on a rainy day. When we were finished washing, we had to empty the tubs and washer, again by carrying buckets, usually to the garden to water the vegetables. Then bring in the wash and get it ready for ironing.

My mother grew up in a world that demanded hard and almost constant physical work from chopping kindling and making up the fire before being able to cook breakfast, to mixing and kneading the bread for the following day before going to bed. She was a healthy woman into her eighties. She was amused at the idea of having to join a gym to get exercise. For her, like the centenarians studied in the longevity research, exercise was part of life: walking, gardening, and cleaning. For us it has to be a conscious choice.

The recommendation from researchers is that we move naturally and move more. One of the newest health findings is the danger of sitting for extended periods.[16] It is not as good to work out for an hour a day and then sit for eight hours as it would be to move around at a gentle stroll for most of the day. Puttering beats pumping iron, as it were. The shepherds of Sardinia and the centenarians of Okinawa spend their days walking and gardening, doing their chores: a lifestyle of sustained natural movement. This is a real challenge in our culture of cars and computers. Dr. Snowdon, one of the researchers on the Notre Dame Sisters study, says he is frequently asked how to age successfully. His recommendation is to take up walking or some other sport or activity that you truly enjoy. "Exercise is one of the most reliable ways to preserve cardiovascular health . . . Exercise improves blood flow, bringing the brain the oxygen and nutrients it needs to function well. Exercise also reduces stress hormones and increases chemicals that nourish brain cells; these changes help ward off depression and some kinds of damage to brain tissue."[17]

Walking and Prayer

Walking is the most natural exercise of all. Walking is the background of the gospels. We have stories of Jesus and his disciples walking around the towns, preaching; and of Jesus sending the disciples off to preach the Good News on foot: "He ordered them to take nothing for their journey except a staff; no bread, no bag, no money in their belts; but to wear sandals and not to put on two tunics" (Mark 6:8-9). There seems to be a natural connection between walking and good thinking, and between walking and praying. Plato and Aristotle taught their students in conversation as they were walking.

Mark gives us accounts of Jesus and the apostles walking and talking, for example: "Jesus went on with his disciples to the villages of Caesarea Philippi; and on the way he asked his disciples, 'Who do people say that I am?' And they answered him, 'John the Baptist; and others, Elijah; and still others, one of the prophets.' He asked them, 'But who do you say that I am?' Peter answered him, 'You are the Messiah.' And he sternly ordered them not to tell anyone about him" (Mark 8:27-30). After the transfiguration Jesus instructs the disciples as they walk: "As they were coming down the mountain, he ordered them to tell no one about what they had seen, until after the Son of Man had risen from the dead. So they kept the matter to themselves, questioning what this rising from the dead could mean" (Mark 9:9-10). They had time to talk this out—it is a big mountain.

Think of Jesus teaching the disciples on the journey to Emmaus, a seven-mile walk, so about two and a half hours' travel time. When the disciples were downhearted and explained their distress to this stranger, Jesus replied, " 'Oh, how foolish you are, and how slow of heart to believe all that the prophets have declared! Was it not necessary that the Messiah should suffer these things and then enter into his glory?' Then beginning with Moses and all the prophets, he interpreted to them the things about himself in all the scriptures" (Luke 24:25-27).

Of course Jesus and his disciples walked—they were poor. But that walking gave them time to talk, and to be in each other's presence (more of a treat for the disciples than Jesus, I think). Walking was a natural part of their world, and the images of the Christian life we have inherited are images of this walk. Journeying along the way has been the most common metaphor we use for the Christian life, or indeed for life itself, which is a journey that always arrives at death. The Israelites' forty-year march through the wilderness to the Promised Land becomes an analogy that Jesus himself takes up: "I am the way, and the truth, and the life" (John 14:6).

Beyond this idea of life as a journey, we find that pilgrimage, walking to special religious places, is something that is found in many religions and cultures. The fathers of the Second Vatican Council described the church as "the pilgrim church, in its sacraments and institutions, which belong to this present age, carries the mark of this world which will pass" (*Lumen Gentium*

48).[18] Part of what the fathers meant to teach us is that earth is not our home, for pilgrims have left their homes to go on this special journey. We know we are headed toward our true and lasting home.

Pilgrimage has given us some of the greatest literature we have. The *Divine Comedy* is the story of Dante's journey through hell, purgatory, and paradise. Chaucer wrote the stories his Canterbury pilgrims told to each other to pass the time as they walked from London to Canterbury. John Bunyan's *Pilgrim's Progress* tells of Christian making his way to the Celestial City, a journey that becomes a pattern of life for the March girls in *Little Women*. Going on pilgrimage to a religious shrine takes us out of our comfort zone, and away from the familiar: "The peaceful and harmonious mixture of peoples from all classes, ethnicities and races which gather together at the pilgrimage site can certainly be an image and foretaste of the ideal humanity of the future"[19]—this is one of the great spiritual gifts of pilgrimage. I remember walking the Holy Mile at Walsingham, in the middle of the crowd of people, hearing the rosary intoned by a thick Irish accent and a Jamaican lilt from different parts of the crowd. At the same time the Poles were praying in Polish, and we all walked together in peace.

Even if we are not on pilgrimage, we can walk and pray. Bernard Basset, an English Jesuit, reminded us that wonder is the beginning of worship, and so recommended walking at night under the stars to pray. Obviously this method is not suited to saying prayers that require a book, but it is a way of praying the rosary, or meditating on a Bible verse or two, or just talking to God. There is something about the motion of walking that allows us to focus on the goodness of creation and connect with the Creator. The first principle of the spiritual life is "be where you are and do what you are doing": excellent advice to make our time of walking a time of prayer. It is in the present moment that we meet God.

We need to rediscover the joys of walking. Our suburbs are designed around the car, not the pedestrian. We have lost the European custom of a stroll after a meal to promote digestion, and also lost the side benefits of a prolonged conversation, stress reduction, and better health because of moderate activity. For our mental, physical, and spiritual well-being, we should lace up our walking shoes.

Practical Steps

We need to build activity into our day. The first step, of course, is deciding that exercise is an important thing to do. Exercise is a great mood improver. I know that if I don't get my workouts or walks, I feel bad physically and emotionally. Conversely, when I am on a regular exercise program, I am a happier person. Lately I am working on building more exercise into my daily activities. I still have much work that requires sitting in front of a computer for hours (writing this book, for example). After an hour with no breaks, I am stiff and have to get up and move around for about five minutes to loosen up again.

Going through the cancer treatment was hard because I had to restrict my exercise. Gradually, though, I got back to walking and doing some light weight-lifting. Then at the three-month post-surgery routine checkup with the oncologist, he found I was in atrial fibrillation. While the doctors were adjusting my medication, I would feel exhausted and breathless. Finally they got a level that kept me stable and allowed me to go back to walking for exercise. Three months later I developed plantar fasciitis, the severe heel pain caused by inflammation of the tendon in the foot. At that point I would watch movies where people were effortlessly walking and envy them. For about a year I was only getting exercise sporadically. It was very hard and discouraging to see how much fitness I had lost.

With good physical therapy, my foot improved and I can walk again for exercise. However, reestablishing a good routine is not easy. I try to walk and/or use the rowing machine three days a week and lift weights two days a week. I need to add in more flexibility and stretching, and figure out how to get everything done without spending my entire life focusing on my exercise program. But this is one of the disciplines of the body that I believe I need to do, not just for my health, but to ensure that I do not use more than my share of medical resources.

All of us adults can improve our activity; there are exercise programs for all levels of fitness, adapted for arthritic knees and painful feet. When we are retired, we have more freedom to do this. Many of the fittest older people I know are mall walkers who go to the mall before the shops open to walk with others. It provides companionship, a safe climate-controlled environment, and no snow—a big consideration for those of us in the Northern states.

Two key elements in this are seeing your doctor to discuss any exercise program, and then finding exercise that you enjoy doing. Explore the possibilities in your neighborhood. Give yourself permission to try new things to find something you enjoy. Many people find activity trackers helpful. C. Everett Koop, formerly our surgeon general, recommended we take ten thousand steps a day for good health. Most Americans walk between eight hundred and three thousand steps a day; when I was working on my dissertation, I was shocked to discover I only walked two thousand steps a day. To get to ten thousand we are going to have to add some walks to our day. I find that if I am wearing my tracker, I do force myself to get up from the computer and walk a bit more throughout the day, which is exactly what I wanted the device to do for me. It also takes the sting out of my memory lapses: now when I have to go back upstairs for the book or the shoes, or whatever I have forgotten to bring downstairs as I intended, I am comforted by the fact I am closer to my daily goal for stair climbing.

If we have been very sedentary, it is wise to start slowly, and set reasonable goals that challenge us and encourage us to be more active without overdoing it. If we rush into a program with unrealistically high goals, chances are we will get hurt and be worse off. Always check with your physician before starting a new program. The best exercise is something you enjoy doing, and building more activity into your day gradually will give long-term benefits. Father Edward, one of the monks at St. Procopius, has bad arthritis; when you ask how he is doing he says, "moving and heating," walking about to ease the pain and using the heating pad when he is sitting.

It can be hard to start and when things interfere, as they will, we can easily decide to drop the whole thing. Here the key is to develop the virtue of perseverance. Let's take heart from a story from the Desert Fathers: Abba Moses asked Abba Silvanus, "Can a man every day make a beginning of the good life?" Abba Silvanus answered, "If he be diligent, he can every day and every hour begin the good life again."[20]

Exercise is one half the prescription for proper care of our bodies; the next chapter looks at the other half, eating.

CHAPTER 3

Eat Less but Eat Right

We in the developed world have an unprecedented problem: too much food. Unlike the generations before us, for whom famine was always a possibility, we are facing an epidemic of obesity with its related diseases. At the same time, there are still many parts of the world and indeed in America where children go hungry and people are food insecure. In the developed world we have also managed to produce a diet that can result in people being both undernourished and obese. Finally, thirty-three million tons of food are wasted each year in America.[1] Pope Francis, echoing the teaching of St. Basil the Great, tells us that the food we waste is stolen from the poor.[2] Clearly, we need to think about food in a different way and change our habits.

Longevity research shows that the healthy centenarians have a habit of not overeating, and of stopping their eating before they feel quite full. This is certainly a contrast to current American practice of supersized meals and huge sweetened drinks. I admit right now that I have trouble with this recommendation. I really enjoy good food, and come from a long line of cooks who always prepare enough in case the entire neighborhood should drop by for dinner. Heaven forbid that we ever run out of food. Our impulse to hospitality is good, but only if the food we prepare doesn't go to waste.

How, what, and when we eat is a cultural marker, an expression of family tradition, like Sunday dinner together, and of our situation in life, like the student eating pot noodles or peanut butter and jelly alone. What we eat shows a lot about our personality, our ethnic background, our religion, our taste buds, and our mental images. Eating puts us into a food system, which raises moral questions: Who has too little to eat? Who is consuming too much? What is our food system doing to the environment, to the people who grow the food and those who harvest it? In *Laudato Sì* (On Care for Our Common Home) Pope Francis reminds us over and over that everything is connected. So how we eat is important not only for our physical health but for our spiritual well-being. As Catholics, eating is at the heart of our religion: at the Eucharist we eat and drink Christ's Body and Blood under the appearance of the bread and wine.

The church has a long tradition of respecting food, in both feasts and fasts. We must eat in order to live, so the appetite for food can easily get out of hand. Gluttony, like lust, is one of the seven deadly sins. To combat these sins of the appetite, the church proposes the virtue of temperance for control of the appetite for food just as she proposes chastity for control of the appetite for sex. When we have our desires under control, we are freed to see our actions in the larger context. When we look at the food system that we are part of, we need the virtue of prudence to decide how and what we are going to eat.

Since the Eucharist incorporates us into the Body of Christ who himself is the fulfillment of Scripture, we begin with food in the Bible, especially the manna in the desert that was the sign of the Bread from heaven that was to come. We look at the rules about food in the Old Testament, and how Jesus gave us a new law in the New Testament. We then turn to fasting and the practice of eating in the Rule of St. Benedict before we move on to the larger food system. The chapter closes with practical suggestions for practicing restraint and developing the virtues of temperance and prudence.

Bread from Heaven

Food is essential to life and we find it involved in the significant incidents of salvation history. Most of the representations of the Fall in our art show Eve offering Adam an apple. The biblical text doesn't in fact say what the forbidden fruit was, but the symbolism of the apple has stayed with us—think of the Wicked Queen offering Snow White the poisoned apple. Because of the Fall, we human beings are wounded. Our desires and our appetites are no longer free; we desire the wrong things, or too much of the good things.

God's covenant, his promise to heal the harm of the Fall, is also marked by food. Originally in the Garden of Eden, God gave Adam and Eve every plant; so they were vegetarian. It is only after the Fall, and the Flood, that God's covenant with Noah includes permission to eat meat (Gen 9:3). This is a marked difference, because to eat meat we must kill a living thing, or perhaps it is better to say a sentient thing, since plants are living.

In the great story of liberation, the exodus, food and eating run like a thread through the narrative. At Moses' encounter with God at the burning bush, he is promised that he will lead the children of Israel to "a land flowing with milk and honey" (Exod 3:8). When the Israelites leave Egypt, and have crossed the Red Sea, they are discouraged because they are in the great desert of Sinai. They cry out for food: "If only we had died by the hand of the LORD in the land of Egypt, when we sat by the fleshpots and ate our fill of bread; for you have brought us out into this wilderness to kill this whole assembly with hunger" (Exod 16:3). In answer, the Lord supplies quails and manna, which "was like coriander seed, white, and the taste of it was like wafers made with honey" (Exod 16:31). The manna was to be gathered each day, except on the day before the Sabbath, when the Israelites were to gather a double portion, bake it into loaves, and have it ready for the Sabbath: "Moses said, 'Eat it today, for today is a Sabbath to the LORD; today you will not find it in the field. Six days you shall gather it; but on the seventh day, which is a Sabbath, there will be none' " (Exod 16:25-26).

The manna lasted while the Israelites wandered in the desert for forty years. In the Deuteronomy account Moses reminds them of God's care: "Remember the long way that the LORD your God has led you these forty years in the wilderness, in order to humble you, testing you to know what was in your heart, whether or not you would keep his commandments. He humbled you by letting you hunger, then by feeding you with manna, with which neither you nor your ancestors were acquainted, in order to make you understand that one does not live by bread alone, but by every word that comes from the mouth of the LORD" (8:2-3). This is the passage Jesus quoted when the devil tempted him to turn stones into bread. When the Israelites reached the Promised Land, the manna ceased: "The manna ceased on the day they ate the produce of the land, and the Israelites no longer had manna; they ate the crops of the land of Canaan that year" (Josh 5:12).

This miraculous food is commemorated in Psalm 78: "Yet he commanded the skies above, / and opened the doors of heaven; / he rained down on them manna to eat, / and gave them the grain of heaven. / Mortals ate of the bread of angels; / he sent them food in abundance" (78:23-25). Reference to this idea of manna being the food of angels is also found in Wisdom: "Instead of these things you gave your people food of angels, / and without their toil you supplied them from heaven with bread ready to eat, / providing every pleasure and suited to every taste. / For your sustenance manifested your sweetness toward your children; / and the bread, ministering to the desire of the one who took it, / was changed to suit everyone's liking" (16:20-21).

We, as Christians, see in these texts the foreshadowing of the Eucharist, the Bread of Life. In the Mass for Corpus Christi, the first reading includes the passage from Deuteronomy quoted above. The gospel for the day has Jesus telling the crowds that he is the bread come down from heaven; his flesh is real food and his blood real drink (John 6:51-58). The text uses *sarx*, meaning flesh, not *soma* (body); and *trogo*, which means chewing or gnawing rather than *phago*, which is the more normal and general word for eating. He is emphasizing that we must really eat the body of Christ; "Life bestows itself on mortals as food and drink," wrote Cyril of Alexandria.[3] Jesus is the Lamb of God, recalling the ritual slaughter of animals in the temple. Now on the cross, his death supersedes the old order.

The Eucharist truly is the bread come down from heaven. By eating it we participate in God. As Graham Ward writes, "I eat the flesh of Christ. I take his body into my own. Yet in this act I place myself in Christ—rather than simply placing Christ within me. I consume but do not absorb Christ without being absorbed into Christ."[4] By baptism we are made children of God, and our life should be a loving response to God's gracious action. The Eucharist is the food that sustains us through our life as we seek to become more and more like God. Saint Irenaeus says, "The Son of God was made man so that man might become son of God."[5]

This, our central act of worship, includes gathering, thanking, sharing food and drink, and praising the God who cares for us. Since this is at the heart of our faith, we should recognize how important eating is. It may seem a stretch to connect healthy eating with Mass, but again, as Pope Francis reminds us, everything is connected. The Eucharist is not just about our individual spiritual journey; it is the sign of the bond of the community and the sign of God's desire that all should be one in him. Our religion isn't just about our head, or our spirit; it involves all of us, including our bodies, as we saw in the previous chapter. "The Eucharistic gift reaffirms the materiality of bread and wine, the body and the senses; it affirms humanity and expresses a radical solidarity toward those who hunger and are outcasts (Matt 25)."[6] Because it is the expression of God's love, we who receive it are charged to go and love others. We can do that in many ways, including how we eat. In salvation history the connection between eating and the worship of God is the Jewish practice of keeping kosher.

Keeping Kosher

When the Lord gave Moses the law on Mount Sinai, it included the dietary laws that Jews follow even today. Christians who have been raised on St. Paul's exhortations against the law (e.g., Rom 3:21-31) tend to see the system of Jewish observance of the law, especially the rules of keeping a kosher kitchen, as man-made righteousness. We are free of all that, we think. But Jesus was a Jew. To understand the gospels and the scandal Jesus caused, and to deepen our understanding of food and its connection to faith, we turn to the laws about food found in the Old Testament and developed in the rabbinic tradition. Then we see how Jesus and the early church transformed the understanding of this tradition for Christians.

When a Jewish scholar came to our university to do Midrash —a particular method of the Jewish reading of the Scriptures—

with our students, she said a Jew is someone who keeps the Sabbath, is circumcised, and keeps kosher, that is, follows the dietary laws. Rabbi Harold Kushner has written a guide to Jewish life that makes clear the purpose of all the laws within the larger theological framework of Judaism. Jewish dietary restrictions aren't about hygiene in ancient Palestine as is sometimes claimed, but about the understanding of the human person. For Jews, human beings have free will, and so can choose to be good. Just as the rules about keeping the Sabbath free of work and the commands to give to charity sanctify the acquisitive instinct, so the rules for keeping kosher sanctify the physical appetite for food. For example, Kushner says, there is a Jewish law forbidding eating while standing up. That is what animals do. Human beings sit, offer prayer, and eat at leisure. That law alone, if applied strictly, would help many of us with our tendency to overeat through mindless snacking.

According to Kushner, the Jewish dietary laws "rest on a single premise: *Eating meat is a moral compromise.*"[7] That action requires responsibility, so the law further requires that the animal be slaughtered with the least possible pain and distress. Not all animals are eaten: only chickens, cows, sheep, and fish—no pork or shellfish. There must be no mixing of meat and dairy because Scripture forbids cooking a calf in its mother's milk (Exod 23:19). From these principles the elaborate customs of keeping kosher have developed. Under these rules, preparing and eating food involves mindful consideration and constant reminders of the bounty of God, our duty to thank him, and our responsibility to creation. These customs also formed Jewish culture, keeping Jewish communities together in hostile societies and marking the boundary between the community and those outside.

The Torah also describes times and ways to fast, for example, as purification in preparation for some religious duty, like Moses before he received the Ten Commandments (Exod 34:28),

Daniel (Dan 9:3 and 10:2), and Queen Esther, who asked the Jewish people to fast with her for three days before she approached King Ahasuerus uninvited, at the risk of her life.[8] Fasting also served as a manifestation of mourning, and as an act of repentance and atonement.

Jewish practice recognizes that the physical is a doorway through which we have access to the spiritual. So the practices of cleaning the house, preparing special foods, and dressing up make the Sabbath a special day; equally, the feelings of emptiness and hunger that fasting creates in the body can awaken knowledge of our dependence on God, the desire for repentance, and the spiritual longing to be filled with God.[9] The practices of fasting, feasting, and keeping a kosher home mean that food is a constant connection to God and the spiritual life.

Jesus and the New Law

These are the dietary laws that were followed in New Testament times, and customs about food marked the special nature of Jesus and his ministry. In fact, one scholar says, "In Luke's Gospel Jesus is either going to a meal, at a meal, or coming from a meal. . . . In Luke's Gospel Jesus got himself killed because of the way he ate. . . . If Jesus is the Son of God made flesh, then his incarnation means eating and drinking, and the vulnerability, dependence, and humility that are integral to the human condition of consuming food."[10]

After Jesus' baptism, he flees to the desert, where he fasts and faces temptation (Matt 4:1-11). The first temptation is to turn stones into bread. Jesus replies, "One does not live by bread alone" (Matt 4:4; quoting Deut 8:3). This account reminds Matthew's Jewish listeners of the forty years wandering in the desert, and of Moses' fast of forty days. Jesus and his disciples are criticized for not fasting, and Jesus tells his critics that it isn't appropriate to fast when the bridegroom is present; later his disciples will fast (Luke 5:33-35). As Jesus and his disciples are walking on the Sabbath, the disciples are hungry and so plucked and ate some of the grain in the field; when rebuked by the religious leaders, Jesus replied, "The Son of Man is lord of the sabbath" (Luke 6:5). Jesus eats with outcasts, the public sinners of his day, like Levi, Matthew, and Zacchaeus (Matt 9:9-13; Luke 5:29-32; 19:1-10). He is called a glutton and a drunkard by religious leaders (Luke 7:33-35). He feeds the multitude on five loaves of bread and two fish (Luke 9:10-17). Jesus has the disciples prepare a Passover meal, and he celebrates it with them, at the same time inaugurating the Eucharist (Luke 22:7-23). After his resurrection, when his disciples are frightened, he takes and eats a piece of fish to show them he is real (Luke 24:42-43).

As we see, Jesus transgressed the laws of his day: by plucking grain on the Sabbath, and by eating with the ritually unclean. In the gospels we find the story of Jesus declaring all foods clean:

> Then he called the crowd again and said to them, "Listen to me, all of you, and understand: there is nothing outside a person that by going in can defile, but the things that come out are what defile."
>
> When he had left the crowd and entered the house, his disciples asked him about the parable. He said to them, "Then do you also fail to understand? Do you not see that whatever goes into a person from outside cannot defile, since it enters, not the heart but the stomach, and goes out into the sewer?" (Thus he declared all foods clean.) And he said, "It is what comes out of a person that defiles. For it is from within, from the human heart, that evil intentions come: fornication, theft, murder, adultery, avarice, wickedness, deceit, licentiousness, envy, slander, pride, folly. All these evil things come from within, and they defile a person." (Mark 7:14-15, 17-23; see also Matt 15:10-20)

In the Eucharist, Jesus tells us to eat his flesh and drink his blood, setting aside the prohibition of eating or drinking blood (Lev 3:17; Deut 12:23). Clearly something new is happening; the old law is being fulfilled by the embodiment of Love itself.

This setting aside of the Jewish dietary restrictions is confirmed for the early church when Peter has the vision of the unclean foods that he is told to eat immediately followed by the appearance of the messengers from Cornelius, a Roman, that is, a Gentile (Acts 10). Peter goes to Cornelius's house and declares, "You yourselves know that it is unlawful for a Jew to associate with or to visit a Gentile; but God has shown me that I should not call anyone profane or unclean. So when I was sent for, I came without objection" (10:28-29). When Peter returned to Jerusalem, he had to explain why he would eat with the uncircumcised (11:3). Peter describes the vision and the voice's command, "What God has made clean, you must not call profane" (11:9). The church accepted that God had saved not just the Jews but the Gentiles too.

This didn't solve all the problems about the Jewish law. The large number of Gentile converts, particularly in Antioch, and the disagreements inside the church over whether or not the converts had to be circumcised and follow the Jewish laws of keeping kosher was finally settled at the Council of Jerusalem (around 49 CE), which sent a letter to the Gentile believers that reads: "For it has seemed good to the Holy Spirit and to us to impose on you no further burden than these essentials: that you abstain from what has been sacrificed to idols and from blood and from what is strangled and from fornication. If you keep yourselves from these, you will do well. Farewell" (Acts 15:28-29). This would seem to end the matter, but theology rarely triumphs over culture that easily. Indeed the disputes continued to rage, and can be traced throughout the Pauline Epistles.

When Paul has returned to Jerusalem to report the results of his journeys, the leaders in Jerusalem want Paul to perform the rituals of purification to show others that he is a faithful Jew: "Join these men, go through the rite of purification with them, and pay for the shaving of their heads. Thus all will know that there is nothing in what they have been told about you, but that you yourself observe and guard the law. But as for the Gentiles who have become believers, we have sent a letter with our judgment that they should abstain from what has been sacrificed to idols and from blood and from what is strangled and from fornication" (Acts 21:24-25). At the same time the leaders are affirming their ruling from the Council of Jerusalem; they are requiring Paul to go through the Jewish ritual actions to prove he is faithful to the law.

As we know, Paul's doctrine of freedom from the dictates of the law prevailed—and gave us much of his theological writing, which can be so hard to understand. We are free from the restrictions of the Torah about what we should and should not eat, but we are bound by the law of love:

> Let us therefore no longer pass judgment on one another, but resolve instead never to put a stumbling block or hindrance in the way of another. I know and am persuaded in the Lord Jesus that nothing is unclean in itself; but it is unclean for anyone who thinks it unclean. If your brother or sister is being injured by what you eat, you are no longer walking in love. Do not let what you eat cause the ruin of one for whom Christ died. So do not let your good be spoken of as evil. For the kingdom of God is not food and drink but righteousness and peace and joy in the Holy Spirit. The one who thus serves Christ is acceptable to God and has human approval. Let us then pursue what makes for peace and for mutual upbuilding. Do not, for the sake of food, destroy the work of God. Everything is indeed clean, but it is wrong for you to make others fall by what you eat; it is good not to eat meat or drink wine or do anything that makes your brother or sister stumble. (Rom 14:13-21)

Paul has highlighted the essential principle of Christian life: all of our actions are to be ruled by love, by our focus on God and on the good of our neighbor. Our religious belief must show itself in our charity and loving-kindness to others, including our choices about eating.

Fasting

Although the church rejected the Jewish dietary law, Christians did keep the custom of fasting. The tradition of ascesis, voluntary fasting and other disciplines, developed very early in the lives of those who left everything to seek God, and continues to this day. "The purpose of ascesis is to divest oneself of surplus weight, of spiritual fat. It is to dissolve in the waters of baptism, in the water of tears, all the hardness of the heart, so that it may become an antenna of infinite sensitivity, infinitely vulnerable to the beauty of the world and to the sufferings of human beings, and to God who is Love, who has conquered by the wood of the Cross."[11] It is interesting that in the ancient and medieval world, when food was usually scarce for most of the population, the fasting laws were very strict. The "black fast," for example, commanded that only one meal be taken, usually at sundown, and at that meal flesh meat, eggs, butter, cheese, and milk were prohibited. During Holy Week the fare consisted of bread, salt, herbs, and water.[12]

As time passes, these laws are gradually relaxed. Today, in a society with an abundance of food, at least in most parts of the world, the tradition of fasting and abstinence has all but disappeared for Catholics as a corporate religious act. Ash Wednesday and Good Friday are our only obligatory days of fast and abstinence in the United States. At the same time, most people are on a diet of some kind or another and one of the popular plans has the person fasting for two days each week. In other words, we are willing to restrict what we eat and drink to look better in the eyes of those around us, or in our own eyes; but we brush off the idea of restricting food for religious reasons. Practicing moderation in eating is now done for physical health, or to save the planet by having meatless Mondays, but not for spiritual health.

Experience has shown that indulgence in food and drink also encourages other sensual indulgences, so the church has recommended the practice of fasting to gain mastery over our desires. This practice wasn't just about individual discipline; the church fathers linked fasting with almsgiving and prayer. Saint Augustine regarded fasting without giving away what one would otherwise have eaten as an expression of avarice. Fasting must be directed to God and neighbor.[13]

As always, this practice should be carried out in a way that doesn't encourage spiritual pride: "And whenever you fast, do not look dismal, like the hypocrites, for they disfigure their faces so as to show others that they are fasting. Truly I tell you, they have received their reward. But when you fast, put oil on your head and wash your face, so that your fasting may be seen not by others but by your Father who is in secret; and your Father who sees in secret will reward you" (Matt 6:16-18).

Following the Second Vatican Council, the bishops in England and in America decided to drop the obligatory fast and abstinence from meat on Friday. Instead, Catholics were to make individual acts of penance. This change in a lived practice that marked the identity of the Catholic community had far-reaching impact. Compulsory fasting and abstinence was a sign of our identification with the poor and hungry, and of our knowledge that we ourselves are needy before God.[14] It also helped Catholics spot coreligionists in the lunch line. In 2011, the bishops of England and Wales restored the Friday fast and abstinence from meat (vegetarians were to abstain from another food they commonly ate). The bishops explained that this is an easy way to remember to do penance, and can be a sign of witness to the world. The US bishops have considered this, but have not yet taken any action.

Benedictine Eating

Fasting as a law of the church was intended to discipline our unruly desires that have been so wounded by original sin. Gluttony is the deadly sin that describes our disordered desire for food. Chaucer's Parson preaches against it in *The Canterbury Tales*, and quotes Gregory the Great on the kinds of gluttony there are and the remedies for it:

> The first is to eat before it's time. The second is when a man procures food or drink that's too rich. The third is when men partake beyond moderation. The fourth is fastidiousness, great attention to preparing and garnishing one's food. The fifth is to eat too greedily. These are the five fingers of the devil's hand by which he draws people to sin.[15]

Gregory the Great was a monk in the Benedictine tradition, and he has masterfully summarized the principles on eating found in the Rule of St. Benedict. Benedict's basic rule about food was that monks should not overindulge in food or drink. He allowed a pound of bread and a half bottle of wine a day to each monk, even though he wrote, "We read that monks should not drink wine at all, but since the monks of our day cannot be convinced of this, let us at least agree to drink moderately, and not to the point of excess" (RB 40.6). On fast days the monks had one meal, on other days a dinner and a supper. The meal consisted of two dishes, since he recognized that monks have different tastes. He allows extra fruit and vegetables, extra food for the very young and the very old, as well as those who had especially heavy work to do. Food was clearly part of the necessities of living, but it was not to be an occasion for self-indulgence. He requires fasts of not eating till mid afternoon for Lent and other days throughout the year (39).

As usual with St. Benedict, he recognizes the realities of life. Workers need food. He orders that the monk who is to read during the meal is to receive some diluted wine before reading for the brethren at their meal "[b]ecause of holy Communion and because the fast may be too hard for him to bear" (RB 38.10). The kitchen workers of the week receive extra bread and a drink an hour before dinner so that "they may serve their brothers without grumbling or hardship" (35.13). When work is heavier, the abbot shall order extra fare (39.6). Although monks do not normally eat the flesh of four-footed animals, he says it may be given to those who are sick and very weak (39.11). He also explicitly forbids snacking: "No one is to presume to eat or drink before or after the time appointed" (43.18). In short, he has made provision for the members of the community to eat together, and to discipline their desires by not having unlimited access to food and drink.

We can see the importance Benedict placed on eating together in chapter 43 of the Rule, titled "Tardiness at the Work of God or at Table," an interesting equating of prayer and communal mealtimes. He requires monks to be present to say the verse and prayer before meals. The monk who is late, through his own fault, may be reproved twice. If he keeps doing this he is not permitted to eat with the others, and his portion of wine is taken away as well. A similar punishment applies to someone who doesn't remain at table for the verse after meals. One of Benedict's serious punishments for disobedient monks was excommunication. Excommunication for less serious faults means the offending monk is excluded from the common table: "For instance, if the brothers eat at noon, he will eat in midafternoon" (RB 24.6). For more serious faults the monk is excluded from the common table and from communal prayer (25).

Benedict wanted the monastery to be self-sufficient: to grow its own food, thus providing occupation for the monks and supplies to feed guests and the poor. The cellarer of the monastery was to manage all the supplies, and "regard all utensils and goods of the monastery as sacred vessels of the altar" (RB 31.10). The cooking for the monastic community was to be done by the monks in turn, for "[t]he brothers should serve one another" (35.1); however, the kitchen that provided food for the guests had skilled cooks: "two brothers who can do the work competently are to be assigned to this [separate] kitchen" (53.17). In all, Benedict presents a vision of a community that properly values the gifts of food and drink, is mindful about eating, avoids overindulgence, and gives to the poor. It is an excellent model, but hard to follow in our day where the food we eat is part of a global network of producers and sellers.

The Food System

We are part of an industrial food system that has brought an abundance of food to us. It is amazing to think that we now worry about the problem of obesity, especially among the poor in our country, when for centuries the major problem was the lack of food and, as a result, serious famines. However, our cheap and abundant food does not come without costs.

In the past food was seasonal, locally grown, and easily spoiled. Advances in transportation and preservation mean that large numbers of people now can eat an adequate diet. But this processing has a cost. For example, stone-ground flours retain the wheat germ and oils that supply vitamins and other nutrients; these oils, however, mean that the flour will go rancid. Industrially milled flours do not have this problem, but have to add back into the flour some of the missing nutrients, or sell them to us as supplements. Industrial systems rely on standardization; so instead of the large varieties of local crops in the food of traditional cultures, we rely on corn, soy, and wheat, in varieties grown specifically for their ability to be processed. Supermarket vegetables are bred and chosen to look nice, and not get damaged in transit. Single varieties are grown and we lose the natural diversity of plants. Heirloom varieties often are funny shapes, not uniformly colored, not standard, and rejected by the supermarket buyers. Ironically, these varieties have now become a valued part of the "foodie" culture.

In a food system, what we eat affects people who are employed in the industries that bring us our cheap foods. I have my students do a project on foods where they trace a commodity like coffee or bananas from source to supermarket and consumer, and identify the justice issues that arise along the way. It opens their eyes to the labor conditions in less developed countries and the high cost, in low wages and workers' health, that the growers pay to produce our cheap food. After several years of listening to the students' research, I find myself conflicted about many issues of foods. One student came to me and told me that this project was ruining her life: "I am Asian and shrimp is a big part of our culture. I can't eat it anymore because of what I learned about the slavery on the trawlers and pollution on the shrimp farms."

Our decisions about what to eat affect much more than the number on our scale. The environment is often damaged by our intensive agricultural practices. For example, bananas are grown in places with few health and safety rules, and use large amounts of pesticides. The pesticides are becoming less and less effective, requiring larger doses; this creates a dangerous environment for the workers. The large banana we are all familiar with, the Cavendish variety, is under threat from a recent fungal disease. The Cavendish itself was a replacement for the Gros Michel banana, which was wiped out by a fungal disease in the 1920s. Researchers are frantically trying to find a variety that will not succumb to the disease and be acceptable to the American market.[16]

The marketing of food in this system has led to a concentration on "nutrients" rather than on the food itself. This is partly the result of how science works: the scientific method breaks things down into constituent parts to study them. We owe the scientists a great debt for identifying vitamins and minerals, and identifying the various components in food. However, we mistake the small amount of knowledge we have about these things for the whole truth about food. We begin to identify particular nutrients as good or bad instead of eating food because it tastes good. Concentrating on nutrients rather than thinking about food as a natural product means that manufacturers put labels on food to convince us it is healthy, for example, NO GLUTEN or LOW FAT on a candy made from sugar and fruit juice. Both claims are true, but the appeal they are making to the diet fad of the moment may blind us to the fact that candy is a treat, to be eaten sparingly.

The research is difficult and ongoing, with results announced by the news media in sensational ways. This means we are inundated with contradictory advice about diet and health. We have developed a cycle for nutrients similar to our cycle for celebrities. New foods—pomegranate, acai berries, oat bran—turn up as cures for the diseases of aging. We have a standard trajectory: scientists discover that certain foods seem to be correlated with prolonged life or lower incidence of a disease. Soon the food industry has jumped on the bandwagon and everything is touted as being THE LATEST HEALTHY THING! The next stage happens when manufacturers separate the "active ingredient" from the food, and start selling that as a supplement. This is followed by scientists showing that the supplement doesn't have the effect we thought it ought to have. And so the cycle starts again.

Rather than cooks who know how to economically feed a family using the food that is locally available, we have food chemists. The chemists are in the business of making our food safe, able to be transported long distances, and appealing to the senses. They succeed. Snack foods, for example, are engineered to leave a taste in the mouth that sends a signal to the brain to want to eat more. Donuts are created that use the right amount of fat to overcome the body's natural mechanism for limiting consumption of sugar. Eating the Western diet, a diet high in meat and in highly processed foods, leads to "higher rates of cancer, cardiovascular diseases, diabetes, and obesity than in people eating any number of traditional diets."[17] Experience has shown that when native populations who have few of these diseases adopt the Western diet, they start to suffer from the diseases.[18] Moving back to their original diet can help them reverse the metabolic abnormalities.[19] We have food that looks appetizing, tastes good, has a long shelf life, and is available in such abundance that we as a nation are getting more and more obese. To live in this system ethically, we need to develop the virtues of temperance and prudence.

Practicing Restraint: Temperance and Prudence

Chaucer's parson gave advice on how to overcome gluttony:

> Against Gluttony is the remedy of abstinence, as Galen says, but I don't consider that meritorious if done only for the health of the body. Saint Augustine recommends that abstinence be practiced for virtue and with patience: "Abstinence is worth little unless it is willingly done, is strengthened by patience and charity, and is practiced for God's sake and in hope of the bliss of heaven."
>
> The companions of abstinence are moderation, holding to the "golden mean" in all things; shame, which avoids all dishonor; contentment, which seeks no rich foods or drinks and has no regard for extravagant preparation of food; measure,

which reasonably constrains the unbridled appetite for eating; soberness, which restrains excessive drinking; and frugality, which restrains the voluptuous pleasure of sitting long and luxuriously at one's food, so that some people, to have less leisure, willingly stand to eat.[20]

This sermon is as valid today as it was in Chaucer's day. Human nature doesn't change; today we see the same forms of gluttony: the gross overindulgence in food and drink, or extreme fastidiousness. We desire too much food, or we become too choosy about our food.

Temperance

A virtue is the habit of choosing the good, and the good usually lies in the middle. For example, a glutton eats too much food, and an extreme dieter eats too little. People with the virtue of temperance eat a moderate amount of food, and do not become grouchy if a particular food they want is not available; they are willing to eat a substitute. They are the masters, not the slaves, of their appetite.

Temperance is the virtue that Chaucer's parson was recommending; when we have this virtue, we voluntarily limit our consumption of food and drink, don't seek out luxurious and special foods and drink, and consider the costs of what we eat. This must be accompanied by an attitude of gratitude. To be temperate, we first must be mindful. Eating and drinking should not be done mindlessly as we are watching TV or driving our car. This shows the practical wisdom of the Jewish commandment to eat sitting at the table, and eat only after giving thanks. That simple act of saying grace before a meal should be a habit, one that we take with us wherever we eat. There is no need to proclaim loudly, "Bless us O Lord" in the restaurant, but a pause for silent prayer reminds us of God's goodness to us and is a nonconfrontational witness to our faith.

Eating and drinking less than we desire, if done voluntarily to restrain our appetites, is an expression of temperance. Some of the simplest ways to practice temperance are to use smaller dishes, leave space on our plates, make a conscious effort to serve ourselves less, and not put the serving dishes on the table. In restaurants where portions are large we can share our appetizer, main course, or dessert. If we know we have a problem limiting wine or chocolate or desserts, we should seriously think about making this a habit to change, through prayer and mindfulness.

The church gives us Lent and Advent to prepare for the great feasts of Easter and Christmas. In the past, these were seasons with additional fasting or abstinence. We can use these seasons to correct our mindless habits of overeating or drinking. The secular world has "dry January" and "meatless Mondays"—the names are different, but the principle is the same. At certain times during the week or the year, it is good to restrict food and drink.

Prudence

The second virtue that is needed is prudence. If temperance is about controlling our appetite, prudence is the virtue of weighing the risks and outcomes of actions and making wise choices. We need prudence on the social level, when we decide what foods we are going to purchase or not purchase because of the labor, or environmental or other justice issues; and we need it on the personal level, when we decide what is a healthy diet for ourselves.

We are confronting institutional realities that create an unjust distribution of wealth, power, and recognition, and thus push a section of the population to the margin of society where people's well-being or even their lives are in danger.[21] We can be oblivious to the exploitation of the land and people that is involved in our food system, or we can pay attention, and be willing to make ourselves uncomfortable by confronting the realities behind our cheap food. When we see these realities, we need the virtue of prudence to make decisions about how we are going to live. Are we going to limit our purchases of some foods? Are we going to support local farmers?

Some years ago, the Mennonite Church, one of the historic peace churches, published the *More-with-Less Cookbook* to help Christians take action about hunger in the world.[22] The recipes were collected from Mennonites around the world and used more grains and plants and less meat. The idea behind the book was the Mahatma Gandhi quote that has been adopted by many charities: "Live simply so others may simply live." By consciously deciding to eat as ethically and healthily as possible, something we must do to stay alive becomes an avenue to connect with God and our neighbor.

Prudence is the virtue that will guide us in choosing how to respond to the injustices of the food system in our community and the wider world. There are local food movements, which aim to support local farmers who are trying to practice a more sustainable agriculture. Some people like to eat local food because of climate change: they don't want their food to have more air miles than they do. On the other hand, countries in Africa and South America rely on exports of produce for developing their economy. What is the right decision? I don't think there is one answer here; that's why prudence comes in to help us make the judgment call. For example, I drive thirty minutes to a farm stand to buy vegetables in the summer. This can be considered as wasting gas, and adding to pollution. However, I think the value of supporting a local family farm outweighs that. Others may disagree.

There is a similar disagreement about eating seasonal food. Barbara Kingsolver, in *Animal, Vegetable, Miracle*, documented a year when her family resolved to eat what they grew or what was available in the local farmers' market.[23] No more convenience of eating out-of-season produce just because we like the taste. The attraction of seasonal food is that it is fresher, probably local, and a treat because we are not eating it all the time. One way to eat seasonally and support local farmers is to join a CSA group—community supported agriculture. You sign up for a weekly box of vegetables and get whatever is seasonally available. It means that you don't know exactly what will be in the boxes, and may find yourself looking up recipes for kohlrabi. Many shares are larger than two people can reasonably consume in a week, so some CSAs offer quarter or half shares.

On the other hand, having good oranges and other fresh produce available year-round is one of the blessings of living in our society, and I, for one, am grateful for that. Equally, frozen fruit and vegetables have almost as much nutritional value as fresh food, certainly if compared to produce that has been picked, stored, and then shipped. Once again, prudence will guide a decision by taking into account all the factors: Where do you live? What is available? What is your budget? What do you like to eat? In prudential matters there often is not a single right answer. The goal is to ensure that eating is mindful practice, not a mindless activity.

We also need prudence to guide us in our personal food choices. There are so many conflicting admonitions and warnings about healthy eating that seem to change every week so that the idea of eating a healthy diet can seem impossible. In traditional societies, you really didn't need prudence to handle food; the culture dictated the diet and seasons of feasting and of fasting. We don't really need scientists to tell us what to eat. We need to recover the common sense of traditional societies and follow some simple principles. One of the best known summaries of how to eat is Michael Pollan's: "Eat food, not too much, mostly plants."[24] That certainly is compatible with the gift of food in the Garden of Eden. Another way of expressing the same thought might be, "eat food as close to the way God made it as possible." This would mean saying yes to fresh fruits and vegetables, meat, fish, eggs, and dairy, but limiting food that is manufactured. In other words, if you can't pronounce the ingredients in your food, maybe you want to eat something else.

Looking around the world, it is pretty clear that God loves variety, so eat a variety of fruits, vegetables, whole grains, proteins. Another rule of thumb is to eat colorfully: spinach, kale, beets, berries. The colors not only make the food attractive, but they are a sign of essential nutrients. Eating like this is easier when we are cooking for ourselves, rather than eating at a restaurant or fast-food place where we have no control over ingredients or portion size. When I had a young family, my confessor interpreted my "duty to my station in life" to mean that I should not feed the family fast food more than once a week. He showed great wisdom.

Cooking can give us more time to appreciate the gift of food, and gain the satisfaction of producing a healthy, well-prepared meal. For many people who have been the primary cooks, the empty nest may be a time when they want to cut back on shopping and cooking. But cooking at home means we are in control of ingredients and portion size. We don't need a lot of preservatives because we are going to eat it now. We found that cooking for the two of us allowed us to try dishes that I wouldn't have made when the children were home, because I didn't want to hear the complaints. My husband has also taken over much of the shopping and cooking; as a result, both of us are competent in the kitchen and could survive on our own even though we don't want that scenario to occur.

Following the spirit of St. Benedict and having a garden would fulfill the hallmarks of healthy living: gentle exercise, good food (mostly plants), purpose, social connection, and faith. Several food pantries in Illinois, for example, have programs that link local gardeners with food banks so that the food bank's clients, soup kitchens, homeless shelters, children's feeding sites, and group homes can have fresh produce. One such giving garden was tended by members of two local churches. An initiative by The Resiliency Institute "sees a new suburban reality where underutilized and resource intensive lawns are converted into productive and abundant edible forest gardens growing fresh, nourishing fruits, nuts, vegetables and herbs for public consumption."[25] If you have the time, skill, and desire, gardening provides a way to care for those in need in your local community and to link your eating with God's gift of nature and his concern for the poor. It also is a wonderful way to connect with grandchildren and get them involved with the natural world and their communities.

If you are thinking of changing your eating habits, the first person to consult is your primary care physician. It would be helpful to keep a food log for a week or so before you have the appointment. You can spot patterns, and your doctor will have a better idea of what kind of changes, if any, are needed. Many practices have dieticians who will help patients design healthy eating plans suitable for their conditions and budget. This is important because some foods interact with common medications.

Eat to Live

As we have seen, how we eat affects us physically, emotionally, and spiritually: "above all, to be nourished implies being in the care of the cosmos, the earth, family, loved ones and—according to some religious traditions—in divine care."[26] As Catholic Christians, we literally "eat to live" when we receive the Eucharist, the Bread of heaven. I hope this review of our tradition from the Bible and daily life has convinced you that eating should not be a mindless activity. Instead, we should find God in every meal, as we find him in the Eucharist, and aim to follow St. Paul's command: "So, whether you eat or drink, or whatever you do, do everything for the glory of God" (1 Cor 10:31).

Preparing and eating food involves thought and gives us constant reminders of the bounty of God, our responsibility to creation, and our duty to thank him. But how we eat is not just an individual choice; it has far-reaching effects. We need to be mindful of those who do not have enough food, and consider the ethics of the food system. To respect our bodies as temples of the Holy Spirit, we also need to eat in a healthy way. The practice of eating less trains us in restraint, and so long as we perform it with prayer and along with almsgiving, we have moved out of the realm of the diet and into the spiritual realm of love of God and neighbor.

Another essential part of aging well is having meaning, purpose, and social connection. It is to these areas of life that we now turn.

CHAPTER 4

Purpose after Work

I remember when my father retired. He had worked for one company for over forty years, enjoyed his job, and was in good health, but when he was sixty-five he had to retire. It was a real blow to him. He, like the men of his generation, thought of himself primarily as the provider for his family. In addition, he was Pennsylvania Dutch, and among the Dutch, you only stop working when you are dead. Our highest compliment for someone is "she's a good worker." Retirement meant that Dad had lost his sense of purpose in life for a time. He thought the idea of retirement as a time to relax, kick back, and enjoy life was not a meaningful life, especially for a Christian.

Dad was onto something. Research into stress has found that a life with little or no stress is often a life of little or no meaning. People are happier when busier and the increased risk of depression in retirement may come from the dramatic decrease in busyness that retirees experience.[1] Psychologists have discovered the "stress paradox": high levels of stress are associated with both distress *and* well-being, while trying to avoid stress ends up creating more stress and depleting the resources to cope with it.[2] Stress challenges us to find meaning in our life, and seems to be an inevitable consequence of having goals that feed our sense of purpose. Stress may even trigger our search for meaning. One of the best books I have ever read was Viktor Frankl's *Man's Search for Meaning*, an account of his experiences in the concentration camps of Nazi Germany, and his observations of humanity under these extreme conditions. His conclusion was that if you have a purpose, a "why," you can endure any situation.

This chapter looks at ways to find purpose for our life. It defines work as activity that demands effort, rather than as what we do for a paycheck, because it is the effort that helps us find meaning and purpose and satisfaction in life. First we look at work in the Rule of St. Benedict, especially the work of God. Then we move on to necessary work on our marriages, work for our family and friends, creative work, encore careers, and close with the Sabbath, a day of rest from work.

Work

"Idleness is the enemy of the soul. Therefore, the brothers should have specified periods for manual labor as well as for prayerful reading" (RB 48.1). Saint Benedict knew that human beings need to work, to put effort into some activity, to have a meaningful life. His Rule was revolutionary in that it asked all the monks to work; in his society manual labor was done by slaves and poor people. He envisioned the monastery as being a self-sufficient community that would also provide for travelers and the poor. So he decreed that the monks, no matter if they were from rich or poor families, do the work necessary to sustain the life of the monastery whether in the fields growing food, in the scriptorium copying books, in the study teaching the children who came to the monastery for education, in the infirmary caring for the sick, or in the guesthouse offering hospitality to travelers. As anyone who has lived on a farm or kept a house knows, the work is endless. His vision was that monks would do all the necessary toil of life but that that toil would be balanced by times for prayer, reading, and resting. This pattern of balance between prayer, work, and rest is a mark of Benedictine communities.

Saint Benedict's vision may have inspired Thomas More (whom you may know from the film *A Man for All Seasons*). More lived in the sixteenth century before mass production, when work filled most peoples' days and they had little leisure. He wrote a description of an ideal society in *Utopia* that is very similar to the life of a Benedictine monastery. For his ideal world, he prescribed that the work of the society be done in six-hour workdays. This was possible because he envisioned a society in which consumption was limited to necessities: all clothing was the same, no jewelry or ornamentation was allowed. This created free time since the economy needed to supply limited goods.

We live in a society that is the opposite of Benedict and More's ideal. Our media and advertisements tell us that we can buy our way to happiness. The economy is measured by GDP: how much stuff we make and buy. It is an age of unbridled, very conspicuous consumption. As we get caught up in this, we work longer and longer hours to afford all the things we think we need for the good life: a large house, fancy cars, designer clothing. Leisure becomes not rest, but just another market where relaxation can be bought and sold as a status symbol: lying on the beach in Tahiti is presented as better than lying on the beach in New Jersey. Shopping is described as a hobby and we are surrounded by devices that teach us to relax by buying more stuff. Pope Francis calls this "a throwaway culture which affects the excluded just as it quickly reduces things to rubbish."[3] In this culture, the ideal retirement is to have nothing to do but to please ourselves. We can entertain ourselves until death.

Andrew Stanton's film *WALL-E* is an extended parable about our throwaway culture and the tragedy of seeking bodily comfort and passive entertainment as the goal of life. In the film Earth is literally trashed; the human beings have left in large spaceships that coddle their passengers. Technology has provided every sort of creature comfort on a physical level; no effort is required to eat, drink, or be clothed in the latest fashion. Entertainment pours out of screens. The turning point of the movie occurs when the captain of the ship rediscovers the need to *do something*—to be forced to make an effort in order to achieve satisfaction. What had been lacking, for the captain as well as the passengers, was any real sense of purpose. To have a healthy retirement we have to expand our definition of work from paid employment to *activity that demands effort*. This is a very broad definition that intentionally includes all the unpaid work of housework, child care, elder care, volunteer work, and many leisure activities. Consider this example:

Two people are digging the garden. Their activity involves effort and skill. If they are digging because they are employed by the landowner, they are working in the usual sense of being employees. On the other hand, our diggers might be homesteaders who are growing cash crops that they will sell for money to pay taxes on the property—they have chosen the labor but they are still working in the traditional sense. But these gardeners might be highly paid executives who are working on their hobby farm where they grow organic food as a luxury, not a necessity; they can buy all the food they need, and so their digging is relaxation. Two minimum-wage workers might be growing food in their time off because they need it for their survival. Is it still leisure? The diggers may be working in the garden because it will supply not only them but also the local food bank with fresh produce while providing them with the healthy exercise they need in their retirement. All of these examples are work—that is, activity that demands effort—but the exact same activity can be either work or leisure; it can be done selfishly or for the love of God and neighbor. Work is more than paid employment and leisure is more than just collapsing on the sofa.

We know from the studies of the exceptionally long-lived that older adults do best when they have some work that contributes to the community and gives them a sense of purpose in societies that have clear shared values. The key may be as simple as not thinking of oneself but of others. Certainly that is the Christian formula for happiness. As followers of Jesus we must take a critical look at what kind of retirement is being sold to us, and make choices that are truer to our values. Since our starting point is loving God and our neighbors, we look for activities that develop our gifts and talents and serve our neighbors.

One of the most important of the many choices we make when we reach retirement age is what we want to do in our life now that we know our time is limited. Today, thanks to legislation forbidding age discrimination, we aren't forced to retire at sixty-five. And, thanks to improved health, many of us can and want to continue working at our jobs, even if we might want to work fewer hours. Moving into this stage of life lets us reorient and balance our lives. We can ask ourselves what dreams are unfulfilled, what we will regret not doing if we were to become sick or die in the near future.

Whenever it happens, the last day at our job marks a big change in our status. In a society that values youthfulness, by retiring we have declared that we are old. Retirement means more than just the fact that we have lost a paycheck; we have lost all the things employment gives us: a structure for our time, a community, a purpose, and personal significance. Losing our identity as a worker in the economy will require some mourning for what we have lost, even as we build a new stage of life. Some kind of work is essential for every time of life. For Jews and Christians, the creation story in Genesis tells us that before the Fall, when the world was in harmony with God, Adam was to tend the garden, that is, to work. After the Fall, Adam toils; his work has become beset with difficulties. But work itself is part of our being made in the image of God who is a Creator.

In baptism every Christian is called to work toward building up God's kingdom here on earth, which is our vocation or call from God. We are responsible for living a life that shows our commitment to Christ and his Great Commandment—love God and love your neighbor—in all parts of our lives. This includes our family, our community, our faith community, and wherever we spend our time in work or leisure. A big life change like retirement is a natural time to rethink priorities and time commitments. We must be good stewards of our time just as we must be good stewards of our financial resources and of the earth. We need to live our love of God through scheduling time for God, for our spouse, for our families and communities but also some time to love ourselves through a healthy lifestyle, time to work at developing our talents, and time to love our neighbors through our actions by working or volunteering.

The Work of God

"First of all, every time you begin a good work, you must pray to him most earnestly to bring it to perfection" (RB Prol. 4). It may seem that one of the privileges of retirement is not being bound by a schedule, but Peter and I found that getting up when we felt like it, and not knowing from day to day what we would be doing, was disruptive, uncomfortable, and inefficient. Even if you don't want to commit to a specific time to pray, it is helpful to structure your day around prayer: in the morning, in a pause between the morning and afternoon, at sunset, and before going to sleep. If you are one of those who wake in the night and have trouble falling asleep, the idea of turning to prayer rather than worry is a healthy one. A similar pattern of structuring a day around times of prayer is laid out in the Rule of St. Benedict, as we saw in chapter 1.

It doesn't matter what form of prayer you choose—whether the Office, the rosary, meditation, or something else—what is important is praying. Make this the first commitment of your time. Just as the Israelites were commanded to give the firstfruits of the harvest to the Lord, we should first set aside time for prayer. I find it necessary to have a regular schedule, first thing in the morning and last thing at night. If I want to go to daily Mass, it had better be on my calendar, or sure enough I will get involved in something and miss it.

Keeping a prayer journal is a way to deepen our experience of prayer and to increase our sense of meaning. Psychologists have found that writing about your values is "one of the most effective psychological interventions ever studied. In the short term it . . . makes people feel more powerful, in control, proud and strong. . . . more loving, connected and empathetic towards others."[4] Saint Ignatius of Loyola recommended the practice to deepen the experience of prayer.[5] Maybe you will write about the phrase that you savored in your *lectio*, or about what you think God is calling on you to do. I would recommend writing by hand if possible; it is a slower process that gives you more time to contemplate the good things and challenges God is giving you in prayer. Having allocated time for the work of God, we can look at the rest of the time at our disposal.

Working on Our Marriage

One of the reasons we set aside time for God is so that he can work within us and our relationships, especially those with our spouse and our family. We can easily think that these relationships do not need conscious attention; after all, we are family. But Pope Francis reminds us that we live in an age of "extreme individualism which weakens family bonds and ends up considering each member of the family as an isolated unit."[6] To combat this tendency and strengthen our relationships we must give the important people in our lives time, attention, and care.

For those of us who are married, the empty nest gives us a chance to revitalize our marriage. Because the years of raising and supporting children to adulthood are incredibly busy, unless we have set aside time to work on our relationship as a couple, we can find ourselves with little common ground other than conversation about the children and the tasks of daily life. So we need to make a conscious effort to set our priorities and goals as a couple for the years to come. If we follow Benedict's advice, we begin this process by praying together, if we haven't already had that as a habit. Even if each of us has a vibrant prayer life as individuals, Scripture reminds us that prayer as a couple is blessed: "Where two or three are gathered in my name, I am there among them" (Matt 18:20).

We need to recognize that in this new situation, conflicts will arise as we negotiate how to live day to day. Many stay-at-home wives and mothers find getting used to a husband who is around 24/7 a challenge. One of my friends said to her spouse, I married you for better or worse, but not for lunch! Recognizing that we each need space and time alone means we can better enjoy our time together. Other friends who are working and finding great satisfaction in their jobs are being pressured by their husbands or wives to retire so that the couple can travel or move to a retirement destination.

These types of conflicts need deep conversation, respectful listening, and humility, especially what Benedict refers to as the second step of the ladder of humility, namely, that we don't love our own will (RB 7.31). We may think that being married for thirty-plus years means we know our spouse inside out, but all of us grow and change. Have the conversations that ask the difficult questions: What is a good day? What is a bad day? What dreams do you have for this time of life? What do you fear about getting older? What will you regret not doing if you were to die next month? I fear the loss of income, even though we have good pension savings. I believe this is a result of growing up when money was tight and my mother had to go back to work during my father's retirement. Fortunately, I found a job I love in a location that gives Peter a chance to retire and do the things he enjoys. We had to negotiate about alone time and boundaries. I love to travel, he doesn't. We agreed to take our dream trip together, and now I travel for work and do more traveling to visit our children. Other times we go together. We share the goal of staying fit, so we respect each other's times for exercise. We also had to renegotiate who did what around the toil of living.

To be independent we must shop, cook, clean, do laundry, and take care of our finances and our living quarters. Much of this is plain toil. It is the transitory nature of housework and yard work that I find so frustrating; we cook dinner today and have to do it again tomorrow. Yet it has to be done. When we retire, we have more time to do these tasks, but we may not have the energy or the physical strength or agility to do them as quickly as we used to. Even if we are in good shape currently, we need to think long-term about our living situation and the work needed to maintain it.

Starting with the most basic needs, food and shelter, we need to make a decision about where we are living. Can we get groceries easily? Are we close to our faith community? What if we lose the ability to drive? Are the house and garden going to take all our time to keep neat and tidy? Are the costs of maintaining this property excessive for a retirement income? Can we simplify and downsize? Would it make sense to move closer to other family members or are we in an established community where we have good social networks? We could spend all our days doing only the necessary toil of living, but that doesn't seem to be a very healthy or a very Christian choice. We should budget our time and our money carefully. If we find we have nothing left to give to others of our time or of our money, we need to rethink our priorities. "Live simply so others may simply live." That is a way to judge the practical decisions we need to make.

We know that there are tasks that must be done to live comfortably, cooking, cleaning, and money management. In many marriages, the partners have split these up and are comfortable with their roles. But in retirement we have time to learn new life skills. If, God forbid, our partner should become incapacitated or die, would we be able to do the work he or she had been doing? It could be a good idea to switch jobs for a period of time. Saint Benedict specified that the monk who cared for the sick and the monk who acts as cellarer (that is, the one in charge of the worldly goods of the monastery) have talents for those jobs. However, he specified that all the monks should take turns performing kitchen service. (He did say that monks skilled at cooking should cook for the guests!) He also had all the monks help each other as needed to get the work of living done.

All of us should be able to fix ourselves a meal, keep our clothes clean, clean the bathroom and kitchen, know when to take the car to the garage for servicing, know who to call when appliances or household systems fail, and budget and pay the bills. If we haven't been accustomed to doing these tasks, now is a time to learn. Maybe you will learn one new job a month, or maybe you will change roles completely for a month. The idea is to learn to do these tasks while your partner is there to explain things. It may be that we find a new interest such as cooking, investing, or gardening. Even though this is the toil of living, it can be done creatively and well, and not just be a chore but a source of satisfaction in our lives.

Working for Family and Friends

After giving time to God and our spouse, we have to look at how much time we have for our family and friends. Pope Francis tells us, "The nuclear family needs to interact with the wider family made up of parents, aunts and uncles, cousins and even neighbors. This greater family may have members who require assistance, or at least companionship and affection, or consolation amid suffering" (*Amoris Laetitia* 187). Although Silicon Valley has given us many new ways of communicating, we still need to spend face-to-face time with those we love. Benedictine monasticism is marked by the communal living of the monks, and their stability or commitment to one monastery. He has his monks come together for common prayer and meals. In fact, he punishes lateness at meals as severely as lateness for prayers (RB 43). There is much wisdom here for our own relationships with family and friends. We can stay in touch in many ways, but it strengthens the relationship when we are together, especially when we are sharing a meal. Pope Francis specifically mentions that not sharing a common meal is one of the challenges of family life today (*Amoris Laetitia* 50).

Our society pushes the ideal of individual households (it sells more stuff), where traditional societies normally see extended families in one household. As retirees, we have to dismiss the advertisers' calls to please ourselves, and instead give our time to building a strong extended family and network of friends, very important for a healthy old age. Many grandparents are taking an active role in caring for their grandchildren, helping the parents in a demanding economy. If we are far from our own grandchildren, can we find ways to give the children in our ambit the most precious gift of all, our time? All of these choices will need to be thought through, prayed over, and negotiated with spouses and family and friends. There is no one way to be family, but we want honest conversations and boundary setting for long-lasting relationships that fulfill our vocation as Christians to love our neighbor as ourselves.

Creative Work: An Experience of the Trinity

The first thing we learn about God in the Bible is that he is the Creator. When we know this we know the answers to the big questions of existence: Where did I come from? Why am I here? Where are we going? The Baltimore Catechism, which you may remember, summarized this well:

> Q. 150. Why did God make you? A. God made me to know Him, to love Him, and to serve Him in this world, and to be happy with Him forever in the next.

These questions and answers give us a wealth of wisdom to contemplate throughout our life. We were made by love for love. God's love overflows into his creation, which was made to reveal the glory of God. We are part of that creation. We bear the image of God and he made us stewards of his creation. We are creators in the image of our Creator. Of course we are not able to make something from nothing, but we can add our mind to what we find in the world and create new things, whether stories and poems or houses and machines.

The Catechism tells us that creation is the work of the Trinity: "In the beginning was the Word, and the Word was with God, and the Word was God" (John 1:1). The Word is God's Son, Jesus. The Holy Spirit is "the Creator Spirit" and the "source of every good." So the Trinity is the central mystery of our faith. It shows us God as love, with his Beloved, the Son, and the love itself, the Holy Spirit. This is one of the most puzzling aspects of our faith when we think about it; it is by definition beyond our comprehension. But who would expect that we could totally understand God? The Trinity isn't senseless, though, just hard to understand.

Dorothy L. Sayers saw that the way we experience being creators is an image or picture of that Trinity. For example, when I make a quilt, I have an idea in my mind of what the finished quilt will look like. That is a human experience to help me understand God the Father, the timeless, unchanging Creator who sees the whole work at once, the end in the beginning. Then I have to cut fabric and sew it; I am incarnating my idea in matter; this is an image of God the Son, who took flesh and lived among us. Finally, when the quilt is finished, other people tell me how they like it, and how they see it. This, Sayers says, is an image of God the Holy Spirit, the active love in our soul that responds to God's love.[7] It is one quilt with three aspects that I experience as a creator. This analogy helps me find a deeper sense of the doctrine of the Trinity. It also tells me that exercising our creative powers is part of loving God.

Sayers was a writer, so she looked at her experience as an artist and saw similarities to anyone who creates. A painter, a writer, a baker, a carpenter, and a dressmaker share an experience of creativity. All of them work with materials to produce something new—whether that something is a painting, a novel, a loaf of bread, a cabinet, or a dress. All human beings have this capacity, even though not all human beings have the capacity, as we usually understand it, to be great painters, sculptors, writers, or artists.

She suggests that we imitate artists in their approach to life. To the artist, life presents a series of opportunities to make something new, rather than a series of problems to be solved. Sayers asks, "How will you proceed to solve a rose?"[8] The flower arranger, the gardener, the painter, and the perfumer are all occupied with the rose itself, respecting its integrity, living creatively. The geneticist, on the other hand, seeks to solve the problem of producing a blue rose. Life involves both kinds of working. In our creating we do need to solve problems, such as the fabric that isn't straight grained, or the wood that has a flaw. But there is a world of difference between treating our work creatively and treating it simply as a problem to be solved.

Much of our paid work is done in the problem/solution mode. There are rules and procedures we must follow. We spend much of our working lives making things fit into the boxes that our employer has designed: claims for reimbursement must include receipts and be a certain kind of expense. Taxes must be paid according to the rules. Our leisure time is also governed by rules: play golf to advance your career, buy these clothes to impress others. The consumer society tells us that any problem can be solved by buying something. This life of work and shopping leaves many people unsatisfied with their lives. Peter Korn, a woodworker and teacher of woodworking, finds that often the people who come to his school to learn the craft feel that normal life leaves some essential part of them unsatisfied. Korn suggests that working creatively "is exactly what generates the sense of meaning and fulfillment for which so many of us yearn so deeply."[9]

When we create, and are focused on our task, Sayers calls it "serving the work."[10] Other writers call that kind of engagement *flow*—the dance of making where we are no longer self-conscious, but so absorbed in the doing that worry about failure disappears and time seems to slow down.[11] This *flow* can be experienced in simple tasks like baking bread, gardening, playing sports, or writing poetry. This experience is exhilarating; once you experience it, you want to do it again! Having work you have chosen in your retirement that will give you a chance to experience flow is a way to flourish.

This experience requires that we put effort into what we are doing, whatever it is. This is hard in a society that values technology for making our lives ever easier. Why work on photography when you can digitally fix your mistakes? Why learn a musical instrument when your phone can play any music you choose at any time? Why read a book when someone has made a movie version? We can live our lives in a world of screens where we won't have to struggle with learning camera settings or fingering or rereading a text to be sure we understand the author. This easy life, though, leaves us unsatisfied; we are missing the chance to be engaged and energized.

Sports are one area of life where you can't phone it in. A screen can help you learn techniques but eventually you have to do something: hit the ball, take the yoga pose, get on the bike. This is another reason (besides improving health) to make some kind of physical activity part of your daily schedule. Many sports also offer the opportunity to engage with others, and be part of a wider social system. Similarly, learning or spending more time on a craft or hobby puts you into a community. These are examples of what one philosopher called practices: activities where we recognize standards of excellence and we bring our efforts and creativity to meet these standards.[12] We become part of a community that says what good photography, or music, is.

Most of us don't think that these activities are part of our Christian vocation, especially since they are fun. However, I believe that these activities are worth doing for two reasons: first, it develops the talents we have been given, and that is an offering to God who *is* Truth, Goodness, and Beauty. We recognize the beauty of an excellent sports performance, a well-performed piece of music, or an exceptional piece of craft work. Participating in that search for beauty is part of our vocation. Even though these activities may be solitary—like playing the piano for pleasure—we are still connected to the larger world of music and God's gift of beauty.

Second, both sports and crafts have a social dimension, and can give us purpose in developing or sustaining communities. One of the happiest invalids I knew was a crafter who suffered for many years with a debilitating illness. She had to be in a long-term care facility, but she used her limited energy to crochet and knit for local charity bazaars and fund-raising events. She found a connection with others through her craft work. This meant that she spent her time thinking of those she was helping rather than dwelling on her own aches and pains, which were many. She was one of the most cheerful people I have known, someone who gave a shining witness to her faith.

Sports and crafts also open up opportunities to connect and give back to our local communities. Youth sports leagues need coaches and umpires; schools and other programs need volunteers and mentors. Working on crafts gives children who have excellent manual skills a chance to shine when, for them, the classroom might be a place of struggle. And, many crafters find community and a source of income or even a second career through their crafting.

Encore Careers

As I said, a major challenge of retirement is losing our paid work and the status it brings. But it is possible that we look forward to retirement from our regular job to begin an encore career, work that we do because we love it, and not just for the paycheck. This idea is showing up in the ads for retirement fund advisors. The ad shows potters, gardeners, and chefs, with a caption indicating their former career as a lawyer, stockbroker, or executive. If we have our health, and the opportunity, we can develop sides of ourselves that have had to take second place during the hectic years of working and raising a family. The new economy of the internet means that it is possible to start small businesses from home, and to find consulting and freelance work in many fields. We who work in the knowledge economy do not face the physical challenges of those who have worked all their life in hard physical labor who look forward to retirement for some rest. We might be ready to switch to something that is *more* physically demanding, or something that uses the knowledge we have gained without the demands of a full-time career.

Peter and I can testify to the satisfaction of such a change; it is invigorating to try new things and get involved with new ventures. There is biblical precedent, too. Abram was an old man when he answered God's call to leave his homeland and follow God to the new land God promised him. In our case I began full-time work in university teaching; I had previously been a part-time instructor. Peter retired from medicine and took up volunteer work that uses his skills in database management and computer programming. The change was good for both of us. Other couples we know have the same dynamic; the wife is working full-time after being at home and the husband is now retired. Retirees with decent savings can start small businesses or take a part-time position that may not pay well but gives them experience in a field they're interested in. One economics professor I know was tired of teaching "the dismal science" and retired from teaching to drive a school bus. He enjoyed driving and liked children. Others, of course, need to find work in order to pay the bills.

Working for the Common Good

For those with financial security, there is a wealth of opportunity in the voluntary sector for work that contributes to the common good and the worker's sense of purpose and meaning. Voluntary work is no longer just making cookies for the homeschool association bake sale or collecting from your street for UNICEF; there are a multitude of organizations that need skilled and unskilled volunteers for many different roles. Retirees are leaving their jobs to join the Peace Corps, for example, or the Senior Corps. Local organizations always need help with a variety of tasks. Organizations that rely on volunteers are an essential part of the safety net for so many people. Giving our time as well as our money is a win-win; we serve and have a sense of purpose and accomplishment, and we help make our community stronger. To begin a search for volunteer placement, you may want to consider visiting these websites:

Catholic Volunteer Network: https://www.catholic volunteernetwork.org

Peace Corps: http://www.peacecorps.gov/volunteer /learn/whatlike/ownwords/1244/

Retired Brains: http://www.retiredbrains.com /senior-living-resources/volunteering/

Projects Abroad: http://www.projects-abroad.org /how-it-works/older-volunteers/

Corporation for National and Community Service: http:// www.nationalservice.gov/programs/senior-corps

Create the Good: http://www.createthegood.org

Points of Light: http://www.pointsoflight.org

Volunteer Match: http://www.volunteermatch.org

Habitat for Humanity: http://www.habitat.org

Some people do not want, or because of caregiving responsibilities cannot commit to, a regular volunteer position; there are always needs that come up in our family and neighborhood that we should see as our chance to be a Good Samaritan. Looking out for our elderly neighbors, or keeping a friendly eye on the neighborhood children—the basic kindness of being a good neighbor is too often missing in these days of high pressure, high speed living. Resolving to be aware of and available to these hidden opportunities to serve is good service and good Christian witness.

The Parish

Your parish will have many volunteer opportunities, but it may not have a fully developed program for people our age.

One pastor told me he was frustrated because despite dropping the age cutoff, he couldn't get people to attend "golden-agers." That didn't really surprise me; we boomers are still convinced we are young. The realities of parish life mean that most activities are centered on the sacraments and sacramental preparation and religious education programs for the young. These always need volunteers. It is up to us as active parishioners to offer to create the opportunities we would like the parish to offer us, whether that be adult faith formation classes or a men's prayer breakfast or a handy persons' group, for example. Most parishes have many groups who are active and need volunteers. Many of us are hesitant to go along and try it out. Perhaps we could decide to spread our wings a bit and find at least one parish activity where we can give our time.

When we are considering how to spend our time, and seeking rewarding activities, we can get overcommitted. I have heard many active retirees say they don't know when they had time to work. We should keep Benedictine balance in mind—prayer, work, and rest—and so we finish this chapter with the idea of Sabbath.

Sabbath

The creation story tells us not only of God the Creator and humanity as bearing the image of God. It also tells us of the Sabbath, a day of rest from work. Sabbath means more than just relaxing; it is a breathing space to find ourselves and reconnect with God and our loved ones. Good rest means a letting go, a resting in the Lord. As wonderful and energizing as work and volunteer activities can be, we also need quiet time. The great temptation in our age is to fill every moment with distraction, especially from screens such as our phones or tablets. I am constantly astonished at how much time I can waste playing games or clicking through web links, telling myself that I am becoming informed about politics. These kinds of activity can be a relaxation, but they can also be a distraction from reality. The Sabbath rest is meant to give us time and space to reconnect with people face-to-face and with ourselves in silence.

Dr. Oliver Sacks writes of the Sabbath,

> And now, weak, short of breath, my once-firm muscles melted away by cancer, I find my thoughts, increasingly, not on the supernatural or spiritual, but on what is meant by living a good and worthwhile life—achieving a sense of peace within oneself. I find my thoughts drifting to the Sabbath, the day of rest, the seventh day of the week, and perhaps the seventh day of one's life as well, when one can feel that one's work is done, and one may, in good conscience, rest.[13]

We can think of retirement as that seventh day of life. We need a change and a rest. Our older bodies don't have as much energy or resilience, and our minds may not be quite as sharp as they were when we were young. It may be that in our lives as parents of teenagers, we spent Sundays at various sporting events, because that's when they were scheduled. In retirement we have a chance to make Sunday a special day. In my birth family, we didn't shop on Sunday. Instead we went to church a lot, sometimes three times in one Sunday. Today Peter and I try to keep Sunday special. I don't answer work emails; we go to Mass and to Vespers at the abbey. After doing this for several years, I look forward to Sunday as a rest from the demands of ordinary life, a sacred space and time to reconnect with myself, Peter, and God.

We may retire from our employment, but as Christians we never retire from bearing witness to the Gospel. Choosing to be active and to work on things that challenge us keeps us using our talents and puts us into contact with others. We can be a witness to everyone we meet by the way we live; that witness of life is the subject of the next chapter.

CHAPTER 5

Witness of Life

In the last chapter we saw how many ways we could find purpose in our lives beyond working for a paycheck. In this chapter we are going to look at our task to be a witness of God's love for us in Jesus. We start with the urgency of this task, by looking at the current statistics on the religious practice of Catholics. We examine what the popes call the new evangelization, an invitation to inactive Catholics to return to an active practice of the faith. Then we turn to the most important way we can witness to our faith—our daily life. All of us are called to live lives that show Christ dwelling within us. People will always compare what they hear us say to what they see us do, so it behooves us to see to it that we make our words and deeds match. Saint Benedict gives us wise guidance on how to do that, especially in chapter 4 of the Rule, "The Tools for Good Works," and in chapter 7, "Humility." Finally, we talk about witnessing to our families, especially adult children who may no longer be active Catholics or who now identify themselves as "nones," those who no longer identify with any religion.

Where Are the Catholics? Not in the Pews

As Christian individuals and as the Catholic community, we are called to share our faith with others. This can seem like a very Protestant idea, but it is true for all Christians, Catholics as well as Protestants, and has been true since the beginning of the faith. Paul was writing his epistles not just to the leaders but to all the Christians in Corinth, Ephesus, Philippi, and the other cities. Over time Catholicism became very institutionally powerful. For those of us who are cradle Catholics, our parents probably grew up in a Catholic "ghetto," a closely knit community where everyone worshiped at the local parish, and most children went to the parish school. Catholicism was in the air, and there was peer pressure to conform. The good thing was that there was a shared religious vocabulary and a community that helped each other live the faith.

If you were raised as a Catholic, you may have noticed that the church is not the same as the one in which you made your First Communion. As boomers, we are defined as those born between 1946 and 1964. Many of us grew up with the Latin Mass, the Baltimore Catechism, and a strong Catholic identity based on the local parish and school. The Second Vatican Council, from 1962 to 1965, seemed to change everything! Mass was now in English, and we sang folk music accompanied by guitars rather than having a choir accompanied by the organ. After the council, the training in the faith that most young Catholics received changed from the familiar certainties of the Baltimore Catechism to a more personal, relational teaching that sometimes sacrificed content for community building. The new openness of the church to dialogue with other churches and other religions seemed to take away the foundation of the way much of Catholicism was lived before the council when we were taught that we were right and the world needed to catch up with us (one of my parish priests referred to ecumenism as you-come-in-ism). It seemed as if instead of the one, holy, catholic, and always right church, it was time to do your own thing.

The sixties also changed culture fundamentally. The old certainties were rejected and the sexual revolution happened. Government was seen as corrupt (Watergate), and we saw the terrible cost of the Vietnam War. Trust in any established institution, including the churches, was being eroded. Beginning in 2002, the truth that some priests were sexual predators who had been moved from parish to parish to protect the good name of the church rather than protect their victims was revealed. Many Catholics feel betrayed by the church and their bishops. A fundamental trust has been broken. All of these factors, plus the new media made possible by the internet, mean that we are in a new religious world. The old loyalties have dissolved. People still hunger for community, transcendence, and meaning, but most who were born Catholic aren't looking to the church to find it.

The fastest growing religious group in the United States is the "nones": the 22 percent of American adults who say that they aren't part of any religious group or tradition. Of those who are eighteen to twenty-nine years old, 35 percent claim no affiliation to any religious denomination. Many in that group are believers in God but they don't regard themselves as belonging anywhere within the world of organized religion; often they say that they are spiritual but not religious.[1] Among US adults who were raised Catholic, 52 percent have left the church at some point in their lives. Of these, 11 percent have returned to the church, while 41 percent of all who were raised Catholic have not returned to the faith.[2] By any understanding of the word, this is a crisis.

Most parishes have responded by building on the idea that Catholicism is inherited: people fall away but then come back to get married and have their children baptized. Much effort is put into the parish religious education program, especially baptismal preparation, and sacramental preparation programs for first penance, First Communion, confirmation, and marriage. However, this only helps those who show up. As we saw from the data presented above, many are simply not coming back for the sacraments.

Maybe, like me, you have adult children who now identify as "nones" despite years of participation in the parish religious education program or in Catholic schools. It is heartbreaking when your child tells you he or she doesn't believe anymore. It can also be a crisis point. Responding to those who now identify as "nones" or as "spiritual but not religious" is a challenge at all times, but especially within our own family. It feels like a rejection of ourselves and our deepest values. Responding in anger isn't going to help; the old proverb about catching more flies with honey than with vinegar is true. What we can do is learn from people who are in the business of talking to those who don't believe.

The New Evangelization

People who are culturally Catholic need to hear the full message of Christ once again. The popes since the Second Vatican Council (except for Pope John Paul I in his very brief time as pope) have made this a priority. The Servant of God Pope Paul VI noted that people in the modern world needed to be evangelized, that is, to be reintroduced to their faith in a way that was relevant to them in their current situation.[3] During his historic 1979 visit to Poland, St. John Paul II coined the phrase "new evangelization" when he proclaimed, "A *new evangelization* has begun, as if it were a new proclamation, even if in reality it is the same as ever";[4] and later he wrote that the new evangelization is, in part, for Catholics who have "lost a living sense of the faith, or even no longer consider themselves members of the Church."[5] Pope Benedict XVI declared the Year of Faith, and created the Pontifical Council for Promoting the New Evangelization. Pope Francis, before he was pope, wrote a document for and with the bishops of South America that called for Catholic Christians to be missionary disciples who joyfully announce the Gospel and work to build a world of justice.[6] As pope he has called the whole church to this work, especially in his apostolic exhortation The Joy of the Gospel.

It is more important than ever that all Christians think of themselves as missionaries and witnesses to Christ and to the hope of the resurrection. This doesn't mean going down the street, knocking on doors, and asking (in the language of Evangelical Protestantism) whether people "know Jesus Christ as their personal Savior." It does mean, however, having a living, personal relationship with the Lord through prayer and participation in the sacraments, and living as someone who knows that each and every person is a beloved child of God. Then God will send us opportunities to work for justice and to share the Good News our neighbors need to hear.

What Is the Good News?

One problem is that many Catholics don't know exactly what the Gospel, the Good News that they're supposed to share, is. They know the gospel as the reading in Mass when we stand up; they have ideas about needing to go to Mass, and praying, and maybe getting ashes on Ash Wednesday. The moral rules are still pretty clear, even if we aren't great at keeping them. But nearly one-third of self-identified Catholics in the United States say that they believe in an *impersonal* God. The Christian story tells us that God isn't impersonal—like "the Force" in *Star Wars*; God is intensely interested in having a relationship with each and every one of us.

I use an acronym when I am introducing the Christian story to my theology classes: C4E. This stands for Creation, Covenant, Christ, Church, End Times. This highlights and helps us remember the overarching story revealed in the Bible that tells us where we come from, why we are here, and where we are going. We believe God *created* everything out of nothing, and not that it was an accidental result of the Big Bang. The Big Bang and evolution may explain *how* life and the universe evolved; God answers the question, "Why is there something rather than nothing?" Human beings aren't accidental products of evolution; they are the image of God. When the first humans sinned, their relationship with the Creator was broken.

The *covenant* is God's promise that he will do whatever is necessary to heal this broken relationship. This began with God's words to Adam and Eve and developed through the Old Testament, as God made his promise that he would not abandon his people known to Noah, Abraham, Isaac, Jacob, Moses, King David, and the prophets.

Christ is the central fact, the turning point of this story and all of history. God loves us so much, he took on flesh and became a human being, Jesus, who lived and died in an obscure Roman province called Palestine. Jesus said he was the Son of God. He preached a God who loved sinners and he described his Father as a shepherd who seeks the lost sheep or as a woman who sweeps the whole house to find a missing coin. He was crucified for his claims. What makes the News really *Good* News is that death wasn't the end of him. On the third day he rose from the dead. He was seen by his disciples; they put their fingers into the wounds on his hands (so yes, his body that had been tortured on the cross is now the body that is glorified). He ate with them, and taught them. After forty days on earth he ascended to heaven, and charged them to tell the whole world that life had changed forever. Death had been conquered and God's promise fulfilled.

On Pentecost, the birthday of the *church*, God sent the Holy Spirit on the disciples, and those cowards who had previously betrayed and deserted Jesus in the hour of his trial were transformed into fearless preachers who told everyone they could that Jesus was God's Son, that he had died and risen from the dead so that we could be like him and follow him to heaven. They no longer feared imprisonment, or torture, or stoning. Nothing could get them to stop letting everyone know that God loves us. The church is his body on earth; it exists to make sure that everyone hears and understands how much God loves us. Christ is present in the church in the word of Scripture, in the Eucharist, and in the community of the faithful. Baptism makes us children of God and Jesus' brothers and sisters, part of God's kingdom here on earth.

All of history is headed toward a final fulfillment—this we call the *end times*. This creation itself will come to an end someday and we will experience the new creation where all tears are wiped away and God's kingdom is fully realized.

This is the Good News; Jesus is alive and wants to be our closest friend. "This is my commandment, that you love one another as I have loved you. No one has greater love than this, to lay down one's life for one's friends. You are my friends if you do what I command you. I do not call you servants any longer, because the servant does not know what the master is doing; but I have called you friends, because I have made known to you everything that I have heard from my Father" (John 15:12-15). That's pretty amazing to think about!

Sharing This Story

Sharing this story might sound scary; I know for years I did not want to "share my faith" even as I was teaching religious education classes. I was comfortable with the faith as an intellectual exercise, but I would still rather talk about my sex life than my prayer life. To be honest I would rather talk about neither, thank you very much. However, Sherry Weddell's book *Form-ing Intentional Disciples*, about the state of the church today, struck a chord with me.[7] Dealing with my own family members who now either identify as "nones," as in having no religion, or who have stopped practicing the faith although they still believe, and with the college students I teach who either think they are Catholic but have no idea what that means or have no religious identity at all, I have become convinced that Weddell and the popes are right. All of us need to become witnesses of Christ's love for us. All people deserve to know God loves them.

Sherry Weddell works with postmodern young adults and other alienated Catholics, adapting the work of Don Everts and Doug Schaupp with college students in southern California. Weddell found that their work resonated with her experience as a pastoral minister, listening to people describe their spiritual journeys. Today people who come to an active faith seem to follow a journey across what Weddell calls five thresholds. These five thresholds give a picture of the work of the Holy Spirit in cooperation with the individual:

1. Initial trust—the person has a positive association with Jesus Christ or with a Christian believer or something identifiably Christian;

2. Spiritual curiosity—the person has a desire to know more about Jesus or the Christian faith;

3. Spiritual openness—the person acknowledges that he or she is open to the possibility of personal change and possible belief;

4. Spiritual seeking—the person begins an active search for God;

5. Intentional discipleship—the person makes a conscious commitment to follow Jesus in his church and to change his or her life accordingly.[8]

Weddell usually works with younger people, but she found that many Catholics, even those active in parish leadership, are to be found at every stage of this journey, and that many become ex-Catholics and leave when they have reached stage four, spiritual seeking, because they can't find anyone in their parish who wants to talk about that. As Catholics we have a culture of silence about religion for ordinary people; it's okay for priests and religious to talk about spiritual life, or about Jesus, but most of us are uncomfortable doing that. We support the parish, but sometimes a personal relationship with Jesus seems to be something that is for the spiritual A team, the holy people. We know that we aren't one of those. Other Catholics have a very active spiritual life, through the sacraments and personal prayer, but wouldn't use the words "personal relationship with Christ" because they just aren't comfortable with that language. They have a living and vibrant faith but don't know how to help others who are searching. Spiritual guidance for laypeople traditionally came through the confessional, participation in parish missions, or retreats. Laypeople were the hearers and not the speakers, so we may feel that we are neither called nor competent enough to guide others back to Christ and his church.

The thresholds remind us that this work is God's, and we are the assistants. We aren't in charge of anyone's spiritual journey, but we can be the friend who helps someone along the way. To me, the most important threshold for being a witness is the first, trust. Those who have no religion need to see Catholic Christians who are living and loving the Lord in everyday circumstances without a lot of talk about it. God can use our daily, ordinary life to attract others to himself. It is scary how often something we don't even remember saying or doing makes a big impression on someone else. The story is told that St. Teresa Benedicta of the Cross, Edith Stein, the Jewish convert who died in Auschwitz, was inspired by seeing a woman stop into a church to pray during the workday. The woman was a stranger to Stein, but the woman's action helped inspire Stein's search for the truth of Catholicism. That kind of unconscious witness is within the power of everyone, and it can continue through the end of our life, even when we are sick and dying.

Trust

Trust in Jesus or in a Christian is the first gateway for many people into the spiritual life. That means that we have to be trustworthy. We can sum up the first duty of Christians as "Don't be a jerk." Pay your bills, keep your promises, don't try to make others look bad, and help those who need it. Saint Paul put it a little more strongly: "But now you must get rid of all such things—anger, wrath, malice, slander, and abusive language from your mouth. Do not lie to one another" (Col 3:8-9). It is pretty basic, but, as we know, it can be very hard to do, especially with the difficult people in our lives. As usual, St. Benedict has sage advice for us.

The first word in the Rule is "Listen"—that is the first step to being trustworthy. To really listen to others today, to look at them and pay attention to what they are saying in their words and in their body language, is becoming unusual. Most of the time, we are focused on a screen. Giving others our complete attention tells them we value them as people and we respect them. Of course, we really must be listening to them and not just being quiet so we can think up the next clever thing we want to say. When they tell us things, and we listen and remember what they said, we are on our way to building trust with them.

In the Prologue to the Rule Benedict tells us how we must act: "If you desire true and eternal life, *keep your tongue free from vicious talk and your lips from all deceit; turn away from evil and do good; let peace be your quest and aim* (Ps 33[34]:14-15)" (RB Prol. 17). We must be the person who "*walks without blemish*

. . . and is just in all his dealings; who speaks the truth from his heart and has not practiced deceit with his tongue; who has not wronged a fellowman in any way, nor listened to slanders against his neighbor (Ps 14[15]:2-3)" (Prol. 25-27). Benedict concludes the Prologue by reminding us that though this sounds hard, "as we progress in this way of life and in faith, we shall run on the path of God's commandments, our hearts overflowing with the inexpressible delight of love" (Prol. 49).

He gives detailed instructions for living as a Christian in chapter 4 of the Rule, "The Tools for Good Works" (see appendix at the end of this chapter). "The Tools for Good Works" begins with the Great Commandment, love God with your whole heart, your whole soul, and all your strength, and love your neighbor as yourself. It then moves on to the detailed commands drawn from the Ten Commandments, the Beatitudes, the spiritual and corporal works of mercy, and monastic wisdom. The list is formidable. It closes with, "And finally, never lose hope in God's mercy" (RB 4.74), which makes me think that Benedict had an idea of just how high a standard he was setting. No one can achieve the perfection Benedict seems to demand; the point is, do we try?

This chapter of the Rule makes an excellent preparation for the sacrament of reconciliation. In our spiritual journey we must move from our unspoken assumption that "God loves me because I am a good person," to "God loves me knowing me as the sinner I am." Our failures are important ways to learn how much we need God, and to get acquainted with our own ego and our selfishness. Trying to live up to a high standard of behavior is one of the best ways to find out how much we rely on God's mercy, which should inspire us to be merciful to others. God is very clear: we must show mercy and forgive others if we want to be shown mercy and forgiven ourselves.

This honesty about our struggles and shortcomings can be one of the best ways to have others trust us and want to speak with us about the things that really matter. We are all living in a society that wants us to look as if everything is perfect; we pretend that we are above failure. This lie extracts a high personal cost. A lie cannot witness to God who is Truth. I have found that admitting to my difficulties and failures has helped others drop their defensive barriers. It worked when I was the mother of young children: apologizing and saying that I was wrong opened up a chance for healing for both me and my children. It is even more important now that my children are adults. And, it does get easier with practice (I get a lot of practice, I have a lot of failures).

Humility

This honesty about our failures and our need of help from other people and from God is a sign that we are beginning to be humble. Humility is based in truth. In chapter 4, "The Tools for Good Works," Benedict gives us a good working definition of humility: "If you notice something good in yourself, give credit to God, not to yourself, but be certain that the evil you commit is always your own and yours to acknowledge" (RB 4.42-43). This virtue is so important to Benedict that he devotes an entire chapter, chapter 7, to it. Humility is the virtue that will make us true witnesses to Christ, and attract others to us.

Benedict had the original twelve-step program. In chapter 7 of the Rule he lays out how to progress in humility:

Step 1: "a man keeps the *fear of God* always *before his eyes* (Ps 35[36]:2)" (RB 7.10).

Step 2: "a man loves not his own will nor takes pleasure in the satisfaction of his desires; rather he shall imitate by his actions that saying of the Lord: *I have come not to do my own will, but the will of him who sent me* (John 6:38)" (7.31-32).

Step 3: "a man submits to his superior in all obedience for the love of God" (7.34).

Step 4: "in this obedience under difficult, unfavorable, or even unjust conditions, his heart quietly embraces suffering and endures it without weakening or seeking escape" (7.35-36).

Step 5: "a man does not conceal from his abbot any sinful thoughts . . . but rather confesses them humbly" (7.44).

Step 6: "a monk is content with the lowest and most menial treatment" (7.49).

Step 7: "a man not only admits with his tongue but is also convinced in his heart that he is inferior to all and of less value" (7.51).

Step 8: "a monk does only what is endorsed by the common rule" (7.55).

Step 9: "a monk controls his tongue and remains silent" (7.56).

Step 10: "he is not given to ready laughter" (7.59).

Step 11: "a monk speaks gently and without laughter, seriously and with becoming modesty" (7.60).

Step 12: "a monk always manifests humility in his bearing no less than in his heart" (7.62).

As laypeople who do not have an abbot to tell us what to do, we need to learn to serve those closest to us. When we read this chapter, my husband and I always discuss step seven, that we should think we are inferior to all. The surface reading seems to suggest that we project a kind of false humility—the "Oh, I am the worst!" where we wait for others to disagree with us. That kind of false humility cannot be what Benedict means. I think Benedict wanted us instead to be concentrating on God and his goodness; then when we think about ourselves we do see how we are a small speck. It only makes God's love for us more amazing.

Step eleven shows us how Benedict is opposed to raucous laughter; in fact the Rule may give the impression that any laughter is unfitting. I believe, though, that he was especially opposed to the laughter that makes fun of others in any way. We know that sarcasm wounds deeply. Benedict wanted us to be humble in our speech; he suggested valuing silence as a first step. As we try to adapt the Rule to our lives, we may find that this is a call to limit the kind of time wasting that comes through, for me, reading political blogs and comment sections. For others it may mean limiting TV time. All of the steps of humility are to help us cast out our pride and selfishness so that our hearts have room for God's love. Humility is necessary for any credible witness to our faith, but especially when dealing with family and close friends.

Witnessing to Our Family

When we are dealing with our own children or other family members, a whole new dynamic of years of events and memories takes over. Priests have told me that they find they cannot minister to their own families. But still they go and try, and we have to do the same. Humility will help us stop the fiftieth replay of the family drama, whatever it is (stupid younger sister, bossy big sister; you're Mom's favorite). It is especially necessary for us as our children are becoming adults. We have to let go of being the parent and let them be independent.

For years, as our children were moving into adulthood, I was still on Mom duty; if they told me about something that was going on in their life, I jumped in with a solution. Eventually, as they were talking less and less about things that were really important to them, I realized that I needed to change. Although I thought I was being loving and caring, the message I really was sending was "you are not grown up and you still need my help." I had to change my script. My new response was "you're an adult, you'll figure it out." The effect was amazing. First of all, I recognized that this was the truth; we had raised competent adults who deserved a chance to make their own life, mistakes and all. Second, after some initial surprise on their part, I found that they were more and more willing to let me into their world. I wasn't judging anymore; I was just listening and expressing my trust in them. I have been so much happier and really enjoy this new freedom and the friendship we now have.

After reading about the thresholds, I am letting go of trying to manage their faith journeys as well. I find this very hard; I was a religious education teacher, and now am a theology professor. But I have to treat my adult children with respect. Instead of focusing on things like "did you go to Mass this weekend," I see that they are making choices that show a deep moral sense, and commitment to truth and justice, no matter where they are on the faith spectrum. I have decided to accept reality and recognize that they have to make their own journeys. It becomes even more important, then, that I am living a life that matches up with what I say my faith teaches.

I am trying to follow how Jesus treated everyone he met: I love *you*; what you're doing, maybe not so much. Jesus didn't tell people how they were sinners. He told them he loved them and that love helped them want to change. Think of his encounter with the woman taken in adultery, or the Samaritan woman at the well. First he accepted and loved them; their response to that love meant that their hearts were converted. This is a healthy model for dealing with the people we meet and it follows the command to judge not lest we be judged.

Pope Francis is calling for us to do this; he thinks it is so important, he instituted a Year of Mercy. Remember how he introduced himself when he was elected pope. At the press conference he acknowledged that many in the room wouldn't be Catholics and he showed respect for them. When he was interviewed and asked, "Who is Pope Francis?" he answered, "I am a sinner." That kind of humility and respect for others is powerful. Its impact went far beyond the church.

The Power of the Hidden Life

Most of us are not called to priesthood or religious life or lay leadership as pastoral associates. All of us are called to be witnesses to Jesus Christ. A model for us who live ordinary lives is Blessed Charles de Foucauld (Brother Charles of Jesus). He was born into a Catholic family, and lost his faith as an adolescent. In adulthood he explored Morocco, where his observations of the devout Muslims led him to ask, "My God, if you exist, let me come to know you." When he returned to France, the warm, respectful welcome he received from his deeply Christian family helped him rediscover God. When he made a pilgrimage to the Holy Land, he found his vocation, to follow Jesus in his hidden life at Nazareth. He lived in the Sahara to be with those who were disregarded by others and said his desire was to "shout the Gospel with his life. . . . I would like to be sufficiently good that people would say, 'If such is the servant, what must the Master be like?' "[9] He was killed by a band of marauders on December 1, 1916.

Although he wrote several rules for religious communities, he concluded that this way of Nazareth was for all Christians. Blessed Charles de Foucauld is a good model for us as we live our ordinary lives, but live them as a conscious witness to our Lord. His prayer of abandonment to God is an example of humility and trust in God. As we struggle with witnessing to those in our families and friends who have lost their faith, I believe this prayer will help us remember that it is God's work, and we have to trust him and do what he commands: love others.

> Father, I abandon myself into your hands; do with me what
>   you will.
> Whatever you may do, I thank you:
> I am ready for all, I accept all.
> Let only your will be done in me, and in all your creatures.
> I wish no more than this, O Lord.

Into your hands I commend my soul;
I offer it to you
with all the love of my heart,
for I love you, Lord,
and so need to give myself,
to surrender myself into your hands,
without reserve,
and with boundless confidence,
for you are my Father.[10]

This prayer will become even more important as we turn to the next section of the book, which deals with sickness, suffering, and death.

Appendix: The Tools for Good Works

[1]First of all, *love the Lord God with your whole heart, your whole soul and all your strength,* [2]*and love your neighbor as yourself*(Matt 22:37-39; Mark 12:30-31; Luke 10:27). [3]Then the following: *You are not to kill,* [4]*not to commit adultery,* [5]*you are not to steal* [6]*nor to covet* (Rom 13:9); [7]*you are not to bear false witness*(Matt 19:18; Mark 10:19; Luke 18:20). [8]*You must honor everyone* (1 Pet 2:17), [9]and *never do to another what you do not want done to yourself*(Tob 4:16; Matt 7:12; Luke 6:31).

[10]*Renounce yourself in order to follow Christ* (Matt 16:24; Luke 9:23); [11]*discipline your body* (1 Cor 9:27); [12]do not pamper yourself, [13]but love fasting. [14]You must relieve the lot of the poor, [15]*clothe the naked,* [16]*visit the sick* (Matt 25:36), [17]and bury the dead. [18]Go to help the troubled [19]and console the sorrowing.

[20]Your way of acting should be different from the world's way; [21]the love of Christ must come before all else. [22]You are not to act in anger [23]or nurse a grudge. [24]Rid your heart of all deceit. [25]Never give a hollow greeting of peace [26]or turn away when someone needs your love. [27]Bind yourself to no oath lest it prove false, [28]but speak the truth with heart and tongue.

²⁹*Do not repay one bad turn with another* (1 Thess 5:15; 1 Pet 3:9). ³⁰Do not injure anyone, but bear injuries patiently. ³¹*Love your enemies* (Matt 5:44; Luke 6:27). ³²If people curse you, do not curse them back but bless them instead. ³³*Endure persecution for the sake of justice* (Matt 5:10).

³⁴You must *not* be *proud,* ³⁵*nor be given to wine* (Titus 1:7; 1 Tim 3:3). ³⁶Refrain from too much eating ³⁷or sleeping, ³⁸and *from laziness* (Rom 12:11). ³⁹Do not grumble ⁴⁰or speak ill of others.

⁴¹Place your hope in God alone. ⁴²If you notice something good in yourself, give credit to God, not to yourself, ⁴³but be certain that the evil you commit is always your own and yours to acknowledge.

⁴⁴Live in fear of judgment day ⁴⁵and have a great horror of hell. ⁴⁶Yearn for everlasting life with holy desire. ⁴⁷Day by day remind yourself that you are going to die. ⁴⁸Hour by hour keep careful watch over all you do, ⁴⁹aware that God's gaze is upon you, wherever you may be. ⁵⁰As soon as wrongful thoughts come into your heart, dash them against Christ and disclose them to your spiritual father. ⁵¹Guard your lips from harmful or deceptive speech. ⁵²Prefer moderation in speech ⁵³and speak no foolish chatter, nothing just to provoke laughter; ⁵⁴do not love immoderate or boisterous laughter.

⁵⁵Listen readily to holy reading, ⁵⁶and devote yourself often to prayer. ⁵⁷Every day with tears and sighs confess your past sins to God in prayer ⁵⁸and change from these evil ways in the future.

⁵⁹*Do not gratify the promptings of the flesh* (Gal 5:16); ⁶⁰hate the urgings of self-will. ⁶¹Obey the orders of the abbot unreservedly, even if his own conduct—which God forbid—be at odds with what he says. Remember the teaching of the Lord: *Do what they say, not what they do* (Matt 23:3).

⁶²Do not aspire to be called holy before you really are, but first be holy that you may more truly be called so. ⁶³Live by God's commandments every day; ⁶⁴treasure chastity, ⁶⁵harbor neither hatred ⁶⁶nor jealousy of anyone, ⁶⁷and do nothing out of envy. ⁶⁸Do not love quarreling; ⁶⁹shun arrogance. ⁷⁰Respect

the elders [71]and love the young. [72]Pray for your enemies out of love for Christ. [73]If you have a dispute with someone, make peace with him before the sun goes down.

[74]And finally, never lose hope in God's mercy.

[75]These, then, are the tools of the spiritual craft. [76]When we have used them without ceasing day and night and have returned them on judgment day, our wages will be the reward the Lord has promised: [77] *What the eye has not seen nor the ear heard, God has prepared for those who love him* (1 Cor 2:9).

[78]The workshop where we are to toil faithfully at all these tasks is the enclosure of the monastery and stability in the community (RB 4).

CHAPTER 6

Accepting Our Cross, Hoping in the Resurrection

So far the focus has been on practices that will help us keep healthy, active, and engaged in our communities. Now it is time to face the unpleasant fact about aging: we fear old age because we know how this ends—for most of us in sickness and dependency and for all of us, in death. We fear losing control, becoming weak, and facing the unknown. According to Maximus the Confessor, one of the fathers of the church, our fear of death causes us to turn our natural energies into destructive passions, especially greed. Fundamentally, greed leads to debauchery, to avarice that produces depression because we are grieved that we cannot possess everything, to envy of others who possess things we desire, and to anger with anyone who prevents us from getting what we desire. Pride begets vainglory, where we display our riches, and anger when others don't admire us.

Human nature hasn't changed. In our day social media with its picture of "perfect" lives has created what we call FOMO, fear of missing out. Death is the ultimate missing out—the final unimaginable change.

As Christians, we have faith that in death, life is changed and not ended. When we lose sight of our destiny to eternal happiness with God, we open ourselves to the fear of death. Saint Augustine wants us to live in truth: "A life without eternity is unworthy of the name of life. Only eternal life is true."[1] We have distorted or silly images of what eternal life means: cartoons of people in white robes standing on clouds, or imagining that heaven is a place where every sensual desire is satisfied. We simply cannot comprehend what being taken into the very life of God in the Trinity is like. Some writers such as C. S. Lewis have given us imaginative portraits of heaven that point beyond the images we understand to the ultimate happiness of seeing God face-to-face. But as comforting as those thoughts seem when we are well and saying our prayers or attending someone else's funeral, it is not comforting at all when we are called back for an additional scan and the technician has just gone out of the room to fetch the doctor. We know the news is not good, and we don't want to hear it.

I was shocked at how unprepared I was for sickness. I am in my sixties; sickness should not be a big surprise. Yet hearing the word "cancer" made the world stop. Plans were cancelled; life became full of doctor's appointments, surgery, radiation treatments. I wanted people to sympathize with me, but I didn't want them to know I was sick, because then I would be the cancer patient or, worse, the cancer victim, instead of myself. It was a roller-coaster ride of emotions. Only now can I appreciate some of the lessons that experience taught me.

When the crisis was over, it occurred to me that I should have had more spiritual resources at my command; after all, I teach theology, including a course that deals with the problem of evil (if God is all good and all powerful, why is there evil and suffering?). There is a wealth of spiritual riches in our tradition about sickness, suffering, and death—not in a morbid sense, but in the context of God's abiding love.

Catholic Christianity never lets us forget suffering and death. The heart of our faith is the Eucharist, in which we are present in the Upper Room at the Last Supper, at Calvary, and at the empty tomb. We begin each Lent with "Remember that you are dust and to dust you shall return." Each year we hear the passion accounts on Passion Sunday and Good Friday. We have the sacrament of the anointing of the sick for serious illness. We dedicate November to the holy souls, a month, in the northern hemisphere at least, that has gloomy weather to match our contemplation of the four last things—death, judgment, heaven, and hell. Most of us have at least one crucifix, a sculpture of a victim of a public execution, on our walls. The church shows us life and death, sickness and suffering, within the theology of the cross and resurrection, which promises that love is stronger than death.

It is often said that our culture conspires to help us avoid thinking about sickness and death. It is hidden away. Yet if we look back at Christian texts from the Middle Ages, we find that people didn't want to think about death any more than we do now. Then as now, what matters is how you live; to have a good death, live a good life. The virtues you develop in life—faith, hope, love, courage—are the virtues you will need when facing sickness and death.

This chapter looks at suffering, sickness, and death in order to help us grow in our faith here and now so we will be prepared for the suffering to come. Many of us are caring for the very old, our parents and others. We need guidance to be good caregivers, to help those we care for face the realities of illness and death. We also need to prepare ourselves for our own inevitable decline and death. To do this we begin by looking at the medicalization of sickness and death in modern American culture and some responses to it. We then turn to our faith, and what the passion and resurrection mean for us. We examine the value of suffering, and the sacrament of the anointing of the sick, which offers us healing.

The Medicalization of Sickness and Suffering

In times past, when people lived and worked in smaller communities where they really knew their neighbors, sickness, suffering, and death could not be ignored. Much illness was attributed to demons, as you can see in the New Testament. Medicine was very rudimentary and hospitals were places to go when you had no hope, and no family or friends to care for you. Most people were cared for in their homes, and so that is where most died. The church was one of the main caregivers for those who were sick. Saint Basil organized a complete city of social services run by monks. It contained a guest house, a hospice, a hospital, and there were free meals and lodging for the poorest workers.[2] Saint Benedict made provision in his Rule for the care of the sick by skilled monks.

Today most of us can live without having to see those who are sick or dying. The advances in medical science and public health—vaccinations, clean water, antibiotics, anesthesia, and advances in medical technology—have given most Americans a much healthier life. We do not fear that our children will die from measles or diphtheria, cancer patients are living longer, and chronic illnesses can be controlled. Today we see people who suffer from serious diseases go into the medical centers and return cured, although now we are also seeing the rise of serious complications from hospital-acquired infections and from medical treatment itself. The hospital has become the place where most of us die, even though if you ask people what they want, many say they want to die at home.

Modern health care is a blessing, and we should be grateful to the men and women who use their talents to make us all healthier. Relieving the suffering of others, whether by feeding the hungry or curing illness, is a duty incumbent on all Christians, and the church provides hospitals that serve their communities with dedicated care from religious and laypeople. But, many of these medical advances are made within a mindset that is foreign to faith. Science, by its nature and methodology, looks for natural answers to natural questions; God is excluded from the experimental method. Pope Francis refers to the modern science/technology mindset in *Laudato Sì*, where he writes, "humanity has taken up technology and its development *according to an undifferentiated and one-dimensional paradigm*. This paradigm exalts the concept of a subject who, using logical and rational procedures, progressively approaches and gains control over an external object. This subject makes every effort to establish the scientific and experimental method, which in itself is already a technique of possession, mastery and transformation" (106).

When the technological paradigm is applied to medicine, the subject is the physician who uses logical and rational procedures. Modern medicine's temple is the hospital where trained professionals use all the technology at their command to fight disease and death. Dr. Sherwin Nuland, a surgeon at Yale, explained how doctors see their work: "The quest of every doctor in approaching serious disease is to make the diagnosis and design and carry out the specific cure. This quest, I call The Riddle, and I capitalize it so there will be no mistaking its dominance over every other consideration. The satisfaction of solving The Riddle is its own reward, and the fuel that drives the clinical engines of medicine's most highly trained specialists. It is every doctor's measure of his own abilities; it is the most important ingredient in his professional self-image."[3] Above issues of value, purpose, hope, love, and meaning, techno-medicine prioritizes technology and technological intervention.[4] This attitude has brought us the great advances in medicine at great costs, both financial and emotional.

The medicalized approach to all sickness, of resisting death by attempting to prolong life for as long as possible, means that death is not seen as a natural part of life but as a failure of medicine—a riddle that wasn't solved. This technological mind-set of problem/solution means that the patient is no longer a subject who is equally involved in the treatment process, but an object, a body or even just an organ, to be treated by the real subject, the physician. This is reflected when we hear a doctor refer not to Mrs. Jones but to the gallbladder in room 313.

When sickness is always treated as an enemy to be defeated, the possibility of death is minimized or ignored. For many years, doctors wouldn't tell patients that their illness was terminal. To them hope meant the chance of a physical cure, so announcing that someone was terminal was seen as killing hope, and claiming more knowledge than all good physicians know they have, since there are always patients who live much longer than expected. The result is that many doctors will try treatment after treatment, chasing any chance, however small, of a cure. Dr. Atul Gawande describes it as having "a multitrillion-dollar edifice for dispensing the medical equivalent of lottery tickets—and . . . only the rudiments of a system to prepare patients for the near certainty that those tickets will not win."[5]

This system harms the physicians and the patients. It demands that physicians do everything in their power to preserve life at all costs while considerations of money, physical comfort, human dignity, and the quality of life experience are, at best, secondary.[6] Medical training focuses on making every effort to diagnose and treat the patient. In many cases this means a prolongation of the process of dying rather than any cure, in the sense of restoring the patient to a good life. Accepting that some patients are not going to get better is very difficult for good physicians. A patient with a terminal illness that they cannot cure represents a major failure.

Patients in this system are no longer full persons. Once they come into the hospital, the routines of that institution and of curative medicine take over. Often patients respond by becoming passive, since that is what the professionals seem to want. This is not psychologically healthy for the patient, who wants to be acknowledged as a suffering person, not just a disease. This system separates cure from healing. Looking for a cure describes the all-consuming urges to fight, resist, and be rescued from sickness and death. Healing is more than this, and may happen even when the sickness leads to death. Healing is the restoration of the wholeness to mind, spirit, and relationships as well as a restoration of coherence to the life story. Patients who participate in healing are those who decide not to be defined by illness but by the meaning they give their sickness in their life.[7]

More and more people see that our medical system is not working; it doesn't provide the healing, care, and meaning that people want. We have highly specialized research hospitals to serve a few while many in our country go without basic health care, and many in the world do not have potable water and immunizations. Modern medicine can prolong the dying process; it has antibiotics for infection, pacemakers and machines to restart a stopped heart, ventilators that can breathe for a patient, and IVs and feeding tubes for those who can no longer eat and drink normally. As a result, death is usually a prolonged and painful event, where the patient is separated from the community and isolated in the hospital.[8]

Although most people would say they would like to die at home, 80 percent of Americans die in hospitals or nursing homes.[9] No wonder many people think a good death is dying unexpectedly in their sleep. This reflects the fears we have of terminal illness: fear of being abandoned; fear of becoming undignified in how we look or smell, or what we do; fear of being a burden; and fear of dying in pain.[10] The fears we have of terminal disease and dependency have led to many calls for assisted suicide.

Dr. Ezekiel Emanuel, a bioethicist and health policy expert, has written that he would hope to die at seventy-five. His reasons are that in great age we are likely to be infirm, and not as creative and active as we had been in our prime. He doesn't want to be a burden, or overshadow his children. To be fair to him, Emanuel does not mean he will take his own life. He is opposed to euthanasia and assisted suicide: "People who want to die in one of these ways tend to suffer not from unremitting pain but from depression, hopelessness, and fear of losing their dignity and control. . . . I have long argued that we should focus on giving all terminally ill people a good, compassionate death—not euthanasia or assisted suicide for a tiny minority."[11]

This system of technological medicine, where patients are subjected to every treatment no matter how burdensome, has called forth the natural death movement, which includes palliative care and hospice. Palliative care focuses on the patient's comfort; it does not seek to cure the problem that is making the patient sick but seeks to improve the quality of life for the patient and the family as the disease progresses. Hospice is the name for palliative services for the terminally ill provided by a multidisciplinary team in the home or in a special facility. Hospice and palliative care seek to disrupt the system that leads to prolonged and painful dying, and restore a holistic experience where the dying person recovers dignity, autonomy, community, and control.

Hospice Care

Dr. Ira Byock, a palliative care physician, explains hospice this way: "We will keep you warm and we will keep you dry. We will keep you clean. We will help you with elimination, with your bowels and your bladder function. We will always offer you food and fluid. We will be with you. We will bear witness to your pain and your sorrows, your disappointments and your triumphs; we will listen to the stories of your life and will remember the story of your passing."[12] Hospice uses a team of nurses, doctors, social workers, and chaplains to help people with terminal illnesses have the fullest possible lives. Hospice workers focus on giving the patient freedom from pain and discomfort while maintaining mental awareness.[13] Hospice use is soaring, yet because it is still feared many patients enter hospice too late to get the full benefits for themselves and their families. And the benefits are very real. A 2010 study at Massachusetts General Hospital compared cancer patients who were either in standard oncology care or in oncology care and palliative care. They found that the group who had palliative care stopped chemotherapy sooner, entered hospice earlier, experienced less suffering—and lived 25 percent longer.[14]

Medicare will now pay not only for hospice care, if you have a diagnosis that says you are likely to die within six months, but also for a visit to your primary care physician to discuss end-of-life options. Dr. Gawande says that "if end-of-life discussions were an experimental drug, the FDA would approve it."[15] In La Crosse, Wisconsin, medical leaders have had a sustained campaign to discuss end-of-life issues and options with everyone who is admitted to a hospital, an assisted living facility, or a nursing home. These discussions ask, at this moment in your life, if you want (1) to be resuscitated if your heart stops, (2) aggressive treatment such as intubation or mechanical ventilation, (3) antibiotics, and (4) tube or intravenous feeding if you can't eat on your own. As a result, the elderly residents of La Crosse do particularly well in the final months of their lives. They spend half as many days in the hospital as the national average, and "despite average rates of obesity and smoking, their life expectancy outpaces the national mean by a year."[16] Sometimes less medical treatment is really better.

Many in the secular world make end-of-life decisions based on their fears of pain, of being dependent on and a burden to others. They have accepted society's idea that values healthy people more than the sick, because the former are contributing to society. This results in a movement for assisted suicide. As Catholic Christians this is not the way we think about these issues. We have a rich tradition that will guide us in our medical choices as we face the end of life. First of all, life is a good, given by God to be treasured and cared for. We are commanded not to kill, and that applies to killing ourselves. However, life is a relative good; there is something better—everlasting life in heaven. So, we can give our lives up as martyrs for the faith, or for the love of our neighbor. Police officers and firefighters make that choice in the line of duty. They are heroes, not wrongdoers even if they are killed. They, like the Lord, have laid down their lives for their neighbors. And we do not have to cling to artificially sustained "life" when we are terminally ill.

Ordinary and Extraordinary Means

In our tradition we use the distinction between ordinary and extraordinary treatment to guide our end-of-life options. Ordinary treatment is morally required in a possibly lifesaving or life-prolonging situation. Extraordinary treatment may be refused or withdrawn. In 1958, Pope Pius XII defined "ordinary means—according to the circumstances of persons, places, times and cultures —that is to say, means that do not involve any grave burdens for oneself or another."[17] Writing about cancer and the possible treatment, the pope reminded medical practitioners of their duty to the whole person: "Before anything else, the doctor should consider the whole man, in the unity of his person, that is to say, not merely his physical condition, but his psychological states as well as his spiritual and moral ideals and his place in society."[18]

Pope Pius reminds us that we are God's creatures and, as such, have human dignity. We do not control our coming into the world, and we must not usurp God's place by deciding on our own death. Therefore, where medical treatment gives us hope of a cure or restoration of function, we are obliged to use it because that respects the gift of life from God. However, we are not obliged to prolong life with medical treatment when a cure is impossible and treatment only prolongs the dying process. So people who have a terminal diagnosis of cancer may choose palliative care, while others may find meaning in accepting experimental treatments that have little chance of working, in order to benefit not only themselves, potentially, but other future patients who may benefit from the research. This can be seen as another way to offer one's life for others. It is a morally praiseworthy act, but it is a free choice, not an obligation.

We can answer the four questions (do you want treatment with antibiotics, CPR, a ventilator, and/or a feeding tube?) using this distinction. So a mother entering the hospital for a scheduled Cesarean section would make different choices from a patient with advanced-stage lung cancer. The mother would almost certainly choose to use all these options; they are likely to be needed only to correct a problem that has arisen during the surgery and will restore her to health. The terminally ill cancer patient may choose to reject all of these treatment options because they cannot cure the underlying disease; they will only prolong the dying process. In all cases we should remember St. Basil's admonition: "Whatever requires an undue amount of thought or trouble, or involves a large expenditure of effort and causes our whole life to revolve, as it were, around solicitude for the flesh must be avoided by Christians."[19]

To make these decisions, it is important to have a physician who is willing to listen to you as a whole person. As patients we must learn to ask questions that doctors can answer. When a new treatment is recommended, ask how many people have had the treatment and how long their lives have been extended. Ask how many and in what ways people become debilitated from the effects of the proposed treatment. Without full knowledge, it is impossible to make a good decision in what is a highly stressful situation. We are fortunate in having seen an example of how to do this in the life of St. Pope John Paul II.

Saint John Paul II

Those of us who are boomers remember the election of this relatively young, athletic pope. We watched as he aged, and suffered from disease, especially Parkinson's. He became an old man before our eyes, allowing us to see him bearing the sufferings of his body. A poignant moment in a public audience when he could no longer speak, and he banged his walker with frustration, spoke immediately to the hearts of all who saw it. This is a man who was suffering, and was carrying his cross willingly. Courage like that comes from the life of prayer that he led. He has given us a contemporary example that we can use to guide us as we navigate the choices that come to us with illness.

Saint John Paul was constant in his defense of life, from conception to natural death. He was as opposed to voluntary euthanasia or assisted suicide as he was to abortion and capital punishment. All violate the dignity of the human person. This defense of life from conception to natural death marks out the Catholic position on human dignity. We have dignity because we are God's creatures; it doesn't matter if we are talented, or creative, or active. It doesn't matter if we are a single fertilized ovum or a comatose Alzheimer's patient: everybody counts. No one is disposable. In his encyclical The Gospel of Life (*Evangelium Vitae*), the pope identified threats against the dignity of the human person: abortion, poverty, human trafficking, and assisted suicide. He understands the pressure that our culture can put on someone who is sick:

In a social and cultural context which makes it more difficult to face and accept suffering, the temptation becomes all the greater to resolve the problem of suffering by eliminating it at the root, by hastening death so that it occurs at the moment considered most suitable.

Various considerations usually contribute to such a decision, all of which converge in the same terrible outcome. In the sick person the sense of anguish, of severe discomfort, and even of desperation brought on by intense and prolonged suffering can be a decisive factor. Such a situation can threaten the already fragile equilibrium of an individual's personal and family life, with the result that, on the one hand, the sick person, despite the help of increasingly effective medical and social assistance, risks feeling overwhelmed by his or her own frailty; and on the other hand, those close to the sick person can be moved by an understandable even if misplaced compassion. All this is aggravated by a cultural climate which fails to perceive any meaning or value in suffering, but rather considers suffering the epitome of evil, to be eliminated at all costs. This is especially the case in the absence of a religious outlook which could help to provide a positive understanding of the mystery of suffering.[20]

In his own illness, St. John Paul accepted medical treatment, including a feeding tube when he had difficulties swallowing. However, as he became much weaker and it became apparent that he had contracted an infection, he chose not to go back to the hospital, and died at the Vatican a few days later.

The Value of Suffering

Saint John Paul is an example of what the church is asking us to do: accept suffering—whatever life throws at us, including sickness, frailty, and dependence on others. Our culture finds this hard to understand. We accept suffering in faith, hope, and love: faith that God is our loving father who will bring good out of evil, hope that desires God's kingdom and trusts that God will bring us to heaven, and love for God and for our neighbors. However limited we are, physically or mentally, we can still choose to accept our state as God's will, and pray with Christ, "My Father, if it is possible, let this cup pass from me; yet not what I want but what you want" (Matt 26:39). We can be like Christ who set his face for Jerusalem, even though he knew that crucifixion awaited him (Mark 10:32-34). He chose to be obedient to the Father, and endure his trial, scourging, and crucifixion. When we accept our suffering and unite our will to God's will, we recover our identity as a free son or daughter of God. Outwardly nothing may have changed; we might still be weak and sick, needing others for our most basic human needs. The world may see a person of no use, but the eyes of faith see a spiritual warrior.

It may seem that Christianity is a religion that loves pain and suffering; it asks us to do as Christ did and lay down our lives for others. Why? The church's attitude toward suffering comes from imitating her Lord. God created us in his image; he wanted us to love him freely. He gave a commandment to be obeyed. But, our first parents chose to love themselves and their own will more than God's will. The Catechism expresses it well: Adam and Eve "become afraid of the God of whom they have conceived a distorted image—that of a God jealous of his prerogatives."[21] Saint John Paul tells us that the original innocence was lost and humanity is now wounded; instead of harmony, relationships are marked by power, lust, and domination. Sin and death entered the world.

Sin has its own logic. Just as virtue builds a habit of choosing the good, sin builds a habit of choosing badly. Sin blinds us to our poor choices and it hardens our hearts. God will not force himself on us; he wants us to love him freely. For many people, suffering and death become opportunities to be shaken out of blindness and hardness of heart. This is not to say that God sends bad things to punish us. God has created a world with order; we can make predictions about natural events, but he has also given us our freedom. As a result, there is natural and moral evil. When the tectonic plates under the ocean shift, we have earthquakes and tsunamis—natural evils, bad things that happen because of the way nature works. When nations allow shoddy construction so that houses collapse in an earthquake and people lose their lives in these events, we have an example of moral evil. The natural evil of the earthquake has caused greater harm because human beings did not seek the common good (good houses for everyone) but their own wants (more profit for builders).

The problem of evil is a real stumbling block for many in our world. People see earthquakes, wars, and other tragedies and ask how there can be a good God who is in charge. Pope Benedict XVI said that many atheists in our world become atheists as "a protest against the injustices of the world and of world history. A world marked by so much injustice, innocent suffering, and cynicism of power cannot be the work of a good God. A God with responsibility for such a world would not be a just God, much less a good God."[22] But the God we worship has revealed himself:

> In him who was crucified, the denial of false images of God is taken to an extreme. God now reveals his true face in the figure of the sufferer who shares man's God-forsaken condition by taking it upon himself. This innocent sufferer has attained the certitude of hope: there is a God, and God can create justice in a way that we cannot conceive, yet we can begin to grasp it through faith. Yes, there is a resurrection of the flesh. There is justice. There is an "undoing" of past suffering, a reparation that sets things aright. For this reason, faith in the Last Judgement is first and foremost hope—the need for which was made abundantly clear in the upheavals of

recent centuries. I am convinced that the question of justice constitutes the essential argument, or in any case the strongest argument, in favour of faith in eternal life. (*Spe Salvi* 43)

As Christians we recognize that there are limits to technological progress and that sickness, suffering, and death are natural parts of this life. There will be suffering, but it need not be senseless or meaningless. God himself, in Jesus, took on flesh and suffered. He is our model, and we are assured that we can unite our sufferings with his for the redemption of the world. That makes it possible for our suffering to be meaningful, if we so choose. Saint Paul told us this was possible: "I am now rejoicing in my sufferings for your sake, and in my flesh I am completing what is lacking in Christ's afflictions for the sake of his body, that is, the church" (Col 1:24). The practice of "offering it up" does this explicitly; the person made a free choice to accept the suffering in the present moment, and offer it to God for the good of the world. This embodies true wisdom for us about our place in God's kingdom. We are not masochists and do not seek out suffering; that would be spiritual pride and just plain foolish. However, we are to accept the cross God sends us and bear it in union with Christ. Benedict XVI says that "offering it up" makes sufferings, great and small, part of the economy of good and of human love (*Spe Salvi* 40). By patiently bearing our sufferings and trials, including facing death, we are accepting the temporal punishment for sin; we are purifying ourselves to make room for God's grace to live within us (*Catechism of the Catholic Church* 1473).

The Sacraments and Healing

We have resources to aid us in our struggles as caregivers or as patients: the sacraments, especially the sacrament of reconciliation, the anointing of the sick, and the Eucharist. We do not have to face illness alone; the prayers and support of the faith community are with us. One of our basic obligations is to ask for the sacraments for ourselves, and to ensure that those we care for may receive the sacraments. When we are in the world of high-tech medicine, hospital staff may be slow to call the priest, as most people see that as a sign that things are not going well. We should insist that the chaplain is called, and draw our strength from the source of life: God himself. We know that the healing we seek is greater than simple cure of the illness.

When Jesus heals, he may or may not cure the illness, but he always restores relationships, including the relationship of the sick person to God. We see this when Jesus returns to Capernaum after teaching in the surrounding villages. A paralytic's friends brought him to Jesus. Jesus tells him his sins are forgiven, which outrages the Pharisees. But Jesus replies, " 'Which is easier, to say to the paralytic, "Your sins are forgiven," or to say, "Stand up and take your mat and walk?" But so that you may know that the Son of Man has authority on earth to forgive sins'—he said to the paralytic—'I say to you, stand up, take your mat and go to your home.' And he stood up, and immediately took the mat and went out before all of them; so that they were all amazed and glorified God, saying, 'We have never seen anything like this!' " (Mark 2:9-12). The Catechism says, "Jesus has the power not only to heal, but also to forgive sins; he has come to heal the whole man, soul and body; he is the physician the sick have need of. . . . [Jesus] did not heal all the sick. His healings were signs of the coming of the Kingdom of God. They announced a more radical healing: the victory over sin and death through his Passover" (*Catechism of the Catholic Church* 1503-5).

As Christians, we must keep this perspective in mind; we should use medicine to heal our sickness. We are forbidden to want to die since that indicates a lack of trust in God. But when we are dealing with a terminal illness as a caregiver or as a sufferer, as Christians we have hope, and must bear witness to that hope in how we handle ourselves in sickness and our dying. We aren't supposed to go it alone; we need to turn to the church for all the help we need. We need this help to face the final things: death, judgment, heaven, and hell. Some of us may remember sermons that used the threat of hell to scare the parish into good behavior, but such preaching has gone out of fashion. The idea of judging someone is anathema to a society that holds tolerance as one of its most important virtues. Yet we should remember the lesson of the judging of the sheep and the goats in Matthew 25: we will all be judged on how we treat others, especially the least, the poor, the suffering, the handicapped, and the dying.

Pope Benedict reminds us that at death we are present before our judge. He tells us, "There can be people who have totally destroyed their desire for truth and readiness to love, people for whom everything has become a lie, people who have lived for hatred and have suppressed all love within themselves" (*Spe Salvi* 45). These people choose their own will, not God's will, and so will find themselves where God is not present, hell. All of us experience places within our lives that we try to hide from the sight of others and of God. We want to appear good and generous and just; but, for example, when a rival gets the promotion we wanted, and our ego is outraged, are we really willing to let God into that rage, knowing that he will tell us to give it up and love that person? I am usually not ready to do that—it will take weeks and months of time and prayer. If we are in the habit of choosing our own will over and over, we exclude God from more and more of our lives. There is a possibility, then, that we will not want God when we have the chance to make the choice.

Equally, there can be people who are "utterly pure, completely permeated by God, and thus fully open to their neighbours—

people for whom communion with God even now gives direction to their entire being and whose journey towards God only brings to fulfilment what they already are" (*Spe Salvi* 45). These are the saints in heaven. Most of us fall somewhere in the middle: we want to love God and we seek him, but we also have sins that are not completely purged. We are saved and we will be in heaven, but first we face a time of purification, which we call purgatory. When I was in a group reading the *Divine Comedy* at Wheaton College, a Protestant evangelical college, I heard one of the participants express surprise at what purgatory is in Catholic theology. She had thought purgatory was a second chance to be saved when we died. After reading the *Divine Comedy*, she understood purgatory as "God's mudroom" where you clean up before coming to the party (you had already accepted the invitation), an excellent description.

Purgatory and our belief in prayers for the dead and prayers to the saints unite this life and the next. Pope Benedict says, "The belief that love can reach into the afterlife, that reciprocal giving and receiving is possible, in which our affection for one another continues beyond the limits of death—this has been a fundamental conviction of Christianity throughout the ages and it remains a source of comfort today" (*Spe Salvi* 48).

The fear of the unknown as well as the fear of judgment and loss of all that we love in this life makes us want to deny death. But since we must face it, we should prepare for it. Medieval Christians had a lively sense of the coming judgment, and had books to guide their preparation. Those guides have much wisdom for us today, which we will explore in the next chapter.

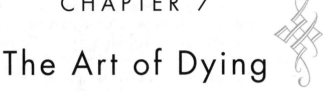

CHAPTER 7

The Art of Dying

Everyone fears death; that is rational, for death is an evil. Wisdom reminds us that death was never God's intention:

> Do not invite death by the error of your life,
> or bring on destruction by the works of your hands;
> because God did not make death,
> and he does not delight in the death of the living.
> For he created all things so that they might exist;
> the generative forces of the world are wholesome,
> and there is no destructive poison in them,
> and the dominion of Hades is not on earth.
> For righteousness is immortal. (Wis 1:12-15)

Death ends our life on earth and leads us to God's judgment. In the Middle Ages, people were no more accepting of death than we are today. However, in the fourteenth century, the Black Death spread through Europe, killing almost one-third of the population. No one could escape thinking about death and the afterlife. In the years following the Black Death, when most people couldn't read, plays could educate about the faith.

Everyman is one such medieval morality play. God commands Death to summon Everyman to his death and judgment. Everyman doesn't want to die. He seeks companions for this journey. Fellowship, Family, Worldly Goods, his five senses (called Five Wits in the play)—all abandon Everyman. He goes to confession, and is reconciled to God and his death. Good Deeds is his only companion as he completes his journey. The play ends with Everyman in his grave, ready to face judgment. As a play, it could instantly speak to an illiterate population, and remind them that all earthly things pass away and it is only what we have done for others that will stand by us at the judgment. It is no accident that in medieval churches, the wall above the exit usually showed a mural of the judging of the sheep and the goats (Matt 25).

Books called *Ars Moriendi*, "The Art of Dying," also appeared. (We would probably call it "Dying for Dummies" or "The Idiot's Guide to Dying.") These were guides to help the dying and their family and friends prepare for a good death. They are interesting, not just as a window into the past, but as a text to educate our own society, which has hidden death away and surrounded it with fear. Many of us say we want to die in our sleep; our ancestors would have been horrified at having such a sudden and unprepared death.

The *Ars Moriendi* books were available in many vernacular languages, with woodcut illustrations to drive the message home for those who couldn't read. There were shorter and longer versions, but for our purposes I want to concentrate on the common content of these volumes. The deathbed was seen as the final battle in the person's life. The devil would be especially active, tempting *Moriens* (Latin for "the dying person"). The medievals were realists; their advice rings true today to anyone who has attended a deathbed. They knew that "mortally ill people themselves do not want to die"[1] so one of the instructions was to avoid giving the sick person too much hope lest he or she would put off the necessary work of preparing for death. The books recommended that the priest be called before the doctor; the patient would need the healing of the sacraments of penance, anointing of the sick, and the Eucharist as much as they needed healing of their bodies.

The first responsibility of the seriously ill is to take inventory of their lives; the books describe the questions the sick person should be asked:

> Do you believe the principle articles of faith, and are you glad to die in unity and obedience with Church?
> Do you know how you have failed God and offended him?
> Are you sorry for your sins and all the goodness you have not done? Do you want to know all your offenses and have special repentance for them all?
> Do you have a firm purpose of amendment if you live?
> Do you forgive those who have harmed you?
> Will you make restitution of goods to those you have harmed?
> Do you fully believe that Christ died for you and you are saved by the mercy of Christ's passion and thank God for it?[2]

These questions lay out for us the proper way to make a full preparation for death. We are required to attend to our obligations to God, our neighbors, and ourselves. This is why the medievals so feared a sudden death; none of this necessary work would be done. Of course, if we reread the list, it is apparent that this is also a good pattern for judging our Christian life when we are in good health. Even with this preparation, *Moriens* would be facing the temptations of the devil in the final battle between good and evil in his life. The books describe five temptations and their remedy. Since human nature has not changed, we will be facing the same temptations on our deathbed.

The Temptations

There are five major temptations, each of which requires a particular virtue to defeat. First there is the temptation against faith. The devil is shown tempting *Moriens* to doubt the faith or to believe heresies. We all "have a great deal of undigested beliefs, [and] unprincipled superstitions" in our life.[3] Serious sickness and the approach of death concentrate the mind and we begin to wonder if what we have believed all our life is true.

The remedy for this temptation is to pray the Creed. Most of us have not fully thought through what it is that we believe, and what the Creed actually means. When tragedy strikes, we start to question our belief in a loving and good God, because it seems as if evil is running the universe. However, saying the Creed will bring us back to reality: Jesus "suffered under Pontius Pilate, was crucified, died and was buried; he descended into hell." We do not believe in an easy Gospel of success, where your faith is measured by your health and wealth. We worship the God who gave his own Son to love us and bear the penalty of sin, death. By his rising from the dead, God has shown that love is indeed stronger than death. The Catechism defines the virtue of faith as the virtue that enables us to "believe in God and believe all that he has revealed to us and that Holy Church proposes for our belief" (*Catechism of the Catholic Church* 1842).

Next *Moriens* will be tempted to despair—to remember all the unconfessed sins committed in life and all the works of mercy left undone, and to doubt the mercy and forgiveness of God. This is a powerful temptation, because one of sin's first effects is to make us blind to our error and offense. The prospect of death suddenly rips off that mask, and we see ourselves and our sins more objectively. We are sinners "who trust in your mercy and love," as the eucharistic prayer states. But, if we have been respectable people, this temptation can be especially strong. In the gospels, the public sinners welcomed Jesus and followed him gladly, because they knew they needed help. It was those who were religious, confident that they were good people, who rejected Christ. We can easily make that same error. Because we don't drink, gamble, sleep around, or run a meth lab, we think we are good folks. When we realize that we are sinners, and how much we need God's mercy and love, it is a blow to our (false) self-esteem. It can be hard to realize that we need God's mercy if most of our life we have secretly been sure that God loves us because we are such good people.

This despair is the unforgiveable sin—not on God's side, but on ours. God is unchangeable love and mercy. When we believe our sin is unforgivable, we refuse to acknowledge this truth about God. He has forgiven us, but we need to repent so that we can know that forgiveness. When we believe our sin is unforgiveable, we cannot repent. So the remedy for this temptation is to look on the cross: have faith, hope, and confidence in God. A woodcut in *Ars Moriendi* shows the saints who accepted forgiveness: St. Peter, who denied Christ three times; St. Paul, who tried to kill all who believed in Jesus; Matthew and Zacchaeus, tax collectors who took their cut from the moneys they extorted; and Mary Magdalene, the repentant sinner. God's mercy covers the big sins like murder and the small, petty sins of jealousy, gossip, and envy that make up our entertainment and politics. But we have to believe in that mercy and repent. We must have the virtue of hope, which helps us desire and wait with trust for eternal life (*Catechism of the Catholic Church* 1843).

One night during a small faith-sharing group in our parish, a woman shared her experience. When her husband was dying, he was very upset and unhappy about how little he had done for the Lord, and how poorly he had lived his life. He was a good man, she said, and a late convert to Catholicism. She arranged for the parish priest to come sooner rather than later to celebrate the sacrament of the anointing of the sick. The effect was healing, not of his illness, but of his soul's distress, and his wife's. She told us that seeing him at peace and ready to die was one of her greatest comforts from that sad time, and a help to her faith ever since.

The third temptation is impatience. This is the "why me?" railing against fate. These books sometimes quote St. Jerome: "Whoso taketh sickness or death with sorrow or displeasure of heart, it is an open and certain sign that he loveth not God sufficiently."[4] This is the temptation against charity, the virtue that enables us to "love God above all things and our neighbor as ourselves for love of God" (*Catechism of the Catholic Church* 1844). This love for God means appreciating that we are weak, sinful, and fallible creatures, and as such we incur temporal punishment due to our sins. The suffering we have in this life can turn us away from God, or give us a chance to practice loving God and accepting our suffering as our cross at this time and place. It can be our purgatory here and now. Christ himself prayed, "My Father, if it is possible, let this cup pass from me; yet not what I want but what you want" (Matt 26:39). So of course we can tell God the truth that we are suffering, and hate it, and wish it would pass, as long as we genuinely pray and mean "not what I want but what you want."

Pope Francis has given us a clear understanding of why and how patience is a sign of love. In *Amoris Laetitia* he writes, "Being patient does not mean letting ourselves be constantly mistreated, tolerating physical aggression or allowing other people to use us. We encounter problems whenever we think that relationships or people ought to be perfect, or when we put ourselves at the centre and expect things to turn out our way. Then everything makes us impatient, everything makes us react aggressively. Unless we cultivate patience, we will always find excuses for responding angrily" (92). The patience we need to accept our sickness is not the work of a moment; it is the fruit of our faith and hope and love of God. However often we fail and become impatient, we can repent and begin again. The saints are not perfect people; they are people who always repent and try again.

The fourth temptation is especially hard for devout and religious people: spiritual pride. The devil, having failed with temptations against faith, hope, and charity, says, "How stable art thou in faith! How strong in hope! How sad in patience! O how many good deeds thou hast done!"[5] This is one of the deadliest temptations. John Bunyan in *The Pilgrim's Progress* notes that there is a way to hell even from the gates of heaven. How do we defeat this temptation? By being truly humble like Saint Antony of the desert who frustrated the devil, "for when I would have thee up by pride, thou keptest thyself a-down by meekness; and when I would draw thee down by desperation, thou keptest thyself up by hope."[6]

Pride is recognizable by its connection with competition and comparison—no one has suffered as I am suffering, no one has done more for the church than I have done. I think our culture encourages this sin, not by messages like "be proud!" but by the narratives that surround us on our screens. Advertisements, news, and drama form us, the viewers, in the habit of seeing ourselves as the star of the show. The truly dangerous temptation is not to think that we are the best in the world, but to believe that we are holier and better Christians than those we live with. We can even be proud of being a sinner. Saint Teresa of Ávila told one of her nuns to stop thinking about herself and her sins so much and to think of Jesus more. That is excellent advice. By keeping our eyes on God, and recognizing our neediness and weakness as God's creature marred by sin, we can become truly meek and humble of heart.

Humility never forgets that each of us is dependent on others. If pride focuses on the quarterback, humility sees that his stats wouldn't be as impressive without a good offensive line. Or pride can focus on the movie star, and miss the writer, the dress designer, the lighting director, the makeup artist, the director, and the surrounding cast that make her stand out. Humility remembers that we are important to God, but not more so and not less so than anybody else. Humility sees that God wants us to be in relationship with him and with our neighbors.

The fifth temptation is attachment to this life: to our goods, our friends and family, our work. This is hard indeed; we are to love our own life, as it is a gift from God. The world is full of the good things he has given us, and we are right to be grateful and appreciative. It is hard to be grateful and detached at the same time. This temptation is really about our thinking that our relationships, or goods, or our work or hobbies are more important than God. The first commandment is that we have no other gods before him. Our attachments are often invisible to us: When does being a good mother cross the boundary into making an idol of our children? or being a good provider become thinking we are indispensable? This temptation is present every day, when we forget that we are dependent on God for everything, and fail to trust that he has our good in mind, even when things do not go our way. When we are terminally ill, however, we face the full force of death: we will be separated from everything in life, our family and friends, our work, our possessions. This is one of the reasons we fear death so. It takes courage to let go, and pray with Christ, "Father, into your hands I commend my spirit" (Luke 23:46). This is harder if through our daily life, we have not built the habit of prayer, saying every day, "Your will be done" and meaning it.

Praying when Suffering

After describing the temptations and the remedies, the books exhorted *Moriens* to follow St. Gregory's advice and think of such things as Christ did dying on the cross, for Jesus was like us in all things but sin. Christ did five things on the cross: he prayed, he cried out, he wept, he committed his soul to the Father, and he gave up the ghost.[7] Christ was active and deliberate in his dying. He took care of his mother, forgave the soldiers, cried out in his pain and suffering, committed himself to God at the time when God seemed most absent, and gave up his spirit. Facing death is hard work, and we are allowed to cry out our pain and give voice to our suffering. The psalms of lament cry to God of pain, distress, and anger. They are truly honest in their rawness. Christ on the cross quoted from one of these psalms, Psalm 22:

> My God, my God, why have you forsaken me?
>> Why are you so far from helping me, from the words of my groaning?
> O my God, I cry by day, but you do not answer;
>> and by night, but find no rest. (22:1-2)

We should be this honest in our prayer. We don't need to use only special holy words; we can give full vent to our feelings before God, trusting that the truth will make us free. We can even pray the cursing psalms, the psalms that call down vengeance on our enemies. This may not be our picture of being a good spiritual person, but it has the advantage of truly opening our hearts to God. We can pray Hezekiah's lament, which reads in part:

> I said: In the noontide of my days
>> I must depart;
> I am consigned to the gates of Sheol
>> for the rest of my years.
> I said, I shall not see the LORD
>> in the land of the living;
> I shall look upon mortals no more
>> among the inhabitants of the world.
> My dwelling is plucked up and removed from me
>> like a shepherd's tent;
> like a weaver I have rolled up my life;
>> he cuts me off from the loom;
> from day to night you bring me to an end;
>> I cry for help until morning;
> like a lion he breaks all my bones;
>> from day to night you bring me to an end. (Isa 38:10-13)

When we have cried out our pain and anger, we have made ourselves vulnerable and open to God's healing presence.

The volumes finished with recommended prayers. The books viewed the deathbed as a place for the Christian community to gather to help *Moriens*. The dying person and friends and neighbors were there to pray on behalf of the dying. One suggested prayer was that attributed to St. Augustine: "The peace of our Lord Jesu Christ; the virtue of His holy passion; the sign of the holy cross; the entireness of the humility of the Virgin Mary; the blessing of all the saints; the keeping of the angels; and the suffrages of all the chosen of God; be between me and all mine enemies, visible and invisible, in the hour of my death."[8] The final recommendation was to say, "into your hands I commend my spirit" (Luke 23:46; cf. Ps 31:5).

Clearly these books were written by those who had seen many deathbeds, and knew the struggles facing the dying person. This can be a guide for us as we are caring for our loved ones, and as we prepare for our own death. We need to have the courage to demand the truth from our medical practitioners. We need to hear bad news not as " 'my time is limited' but 'my time is valuable, too valuable not to capture every moment I can.' "[9] Advance care planning is part of preparing for death that we can do now. It is to these practicalities of that planning that we now turn.

Making Plans

The point of most of this book was to extend the active age as long as possible, but that doesn't mean we can ignore preparing for frailty, illness, and death. We know from the statistics kept by the US Public Health Service that the average life expectancy for us is somewhere in our eighties. If we retire from our main employment at sixty-five, we have about twenty years to live and prepare for our death. We are often called on to be caregivers and decision makers for the very old, our parents or other significant people in our lives. The aim of this section is to lay out the questions that must be considered, and what plans and documents should be organized as soon as possible.

Our retirement years should find us enjoying the fruits of our labors and, as covered in the preceding chapters, being physically active and socially connected, participating in activities that give our lives meaning and purpose, and taking an active role in our faith community. It is our responsibility, while we are in good shape mentally and physically, to prepare for the future. As Christians, we know that means preparing for our deaths. Serious questions need attention:

> Where will I live if I become frail? Can I be cared for in my current residence? Should I move closer to my children or other potential support networks?
>
> Do I have a will and is it up to date?
>
> Do I have my financial records organized and easily available to those who may need to find them in case of a health emergency?
>
> Do I have a list of my social media, online banking, and other passwords made and in a safe place?
>
> Do I have a written expression of my wishes for end-of-life care?
>
> Do I have a health care power of attorney that is current and has designated a health care decision maker who is willing and able to take that role?
>
> Have I discussed my desires for health care as I age and as I face the end of life with my family and my physician?
>
> Have I planned my funeral and written down my wishes so that my survivors will know what I wanted? They will be worn down with grief and faced with so many decisions; it is a kindness to leave them a letter with your wishes spelled out.

These are not fun questions, but dealing with them will allow you peace of mind, and the ability to live your life with assurance that you have made the preparations that are necessary. If you have ever coped with a frail elderly person who has not made these preparations, I believe you will be convinced of their value.

The last stage of life can be the hardest, especially in the high-tech environment of the intensive care unit. However, there are alternatives, such as palliative care and hospice, as discussed in chapter 6. At the point when you need to make the decisions about what kind of end-of-life care you want, you may not be able to do so because of your illness. One of the current tragedies in our health care system is that people do not avail themselves of hospice care early enough to get the full benefit. This is why planning now, and revisiting your wishes with your physician often is essential. This is the time when we will need the spiritual resources we have developed over the course of our life to come to our aid. We especially need an honest caregiver and a physician who will tell us the truth.

At this stage of life, we need to consider the questions from the *Ars Moriendi*: Do we believe in God and what the church teaches? Have we reconciled with those we have harmed, and made restitution? Have we told those we love how much they mean to us? We should be doing these things now before we come to our final illness; reconciliation and peace is a gift God wants to share with us, if we will do our part. At the end of life, when it seems we have the least to give others, we can be witnesses to the faith, hope, and love that God gives us. We can be a part of God's plan for the world, and follow St. John Paul II's example by accepting all things that happen to us as coming from God for our good and the good of the world.

Life Is Changed

People often criticized Christians for promising "pie in the sky when you die," and not working for justice in this world.

That may have been true at one time, but our problem today is that we have forgotten what Christ's resurrection means. Truly, for the Christian, life is changed, not ended, with death. We are destined for heaven. Although we find angels and demons in popular entertainment, we have little that gives us a vision of the glory of God and his kingdom. We have to remind ourselves of the meaning of God's promise that we shall be with him.

We are creatures of time and space, and cannot think ourselves out of them. So we have cartoon depictions of heaven as endlessly sitting on clouds, playing a harp. The Bible uses very pictorial images of heaven, for instance, the new Jerusalem in Revelation:

> It has the glory of God and a radiance like a very rare jewel, like jasper, clear as crystal. It has a great, high wall with twelve gates, and at the gates twelve angels, and on the gates are inscribed the names of the twelve tribes of the Israelites; on the east three gates, on the north three gates, on the south three gates, and on the west three gates. And the wall of the city has twelve foundations, and on them are the twelve names of the twelve apostles of the Lamb. . . . The wall is built of jasper, while the city is pure gold, clear as glass. The foundations of the wall of the city are adorned with every jewel; the first was jasper, the second sapphire, the third agate, the fourth emerald, the fifth onyx, the sixth carnelian, the seventh chrysolite, the eighth beryl, the ninth topaz, the tenth chrysoprase, the eleventh jacinth, the twelfth amethyst. And the twelve gates are twelve pearls, each of the gates is a single pearl, and the street of the city is pure gold, transparent as glass.
>
> I saw no temple in the city, for its temple is the Lord God the Almighty and the Lamb. And the city has no need of sun or moon to shine on it, for the glory of God is its light, and its lamp is the Lamb. The nations will walk by its light, and the kings of the earth will bring their glory into it. Its gates will never be shut by day—and there will be no night there. People will bring into it the glory and the honor of the nations. (Rev 21:11-14, 18-26)

Here is a vision of all that is most precious, an image of glory and radiance beyond adequate description. Other writers have tried to give us this vision—Dante with the *Divine Comedy* and, in our own time, C. S. Lewis, especially in *The Great Divorce* and *The Last Battle*, the last book in the Narnia series. I think these ideas are important to keep in mind, because it is so easy to be trapped by the enticing world around us. But to prepare for our deaths, and to comfort others facing their deaths, we must recover true Christian hope: not that we will be spared suffering, but that we are destined for life with God.

One way to do this is to return to the pattern of prayer that has the acronym ACTS: adoration, contrition, thanksgiving, and supplication. At this stage in our life, adoration of God may mean focusing on his greatness, goodness, beauty, and splendor. We can use the psalms, especially Psalm 8 and 150, or the song of praise of the men in the fiery furnace, Daniel 3:52-90. Contrition will include not only the sins of the day, but also those other sins and faults that come to our mind from the past. We can repent again, and see if there is a way to make restitution. This contrition will help us know ourselves as sinners who need God's mercy. Thanksgiving will be not just for the blessings of the day, but also for the blessings of our life as a whole as we look back on it. Many times we can see new things to be thankful for as our memories bring incidents to our mind. We must also be thankful to be called to live with God in heaven. Finally in our supplications we pray for our daily needs, for the needs of our family and the world, and for perseverance in faith and hope.

We are to love God with our minds and our hearts, so we should be studying God's word and other spiritual writings, such as the accounts of the saints, especially the martyrs. The *Martyrdom of St. Polycarp* is one of our earliest Christian texts, and it is a deeply moving account that gives encouragement that God never abandons us. In our own day, Pope Benedict wrote an encyclical about Christian hope, *Spe Salvi*, that I have quoted from throughout the book. In it he gives us one of the best descriptions of heaven that I have heard:

> To imagine ourselves outside the temporality that imprisons us and in some way to sense that eternity is not an unending succession of days in the calendar, but something more like the supreme moment of satisfaction, in which totality embraces us and we embrace totality—this we can only attempt. It would be like plunging into the ocean of infinite love, a moment in which time—the before and after—no longer exists. We can only attempt to grasp the idea that such a moment is life in the full sense, a plunging ever anew into the vastness of being, in which we are simply overwhelmed with joy. (12)

Suffering will never have the last word; death has been conquered by love. This is Christian hope that comforts us every day, and especially in the hour of our death. This is the purpose and goal of life, and all the practices recommended in this book are designed to help us remember this in a world that wants to forget God. So I will close with the final prayer of Compline: May the Lord grant us a quiet night and a peaceful death. Amen.

Notes

Preface

1. Timothy Radcliffe, "Foreword," in *St. Dominic: The Story of a Preaching Friar*, Donald Goergen (Mahwah, NJ: Paulist Press, 2016).

2. Quotations from the Rule of St. Benedict are taken from Timothy Fry, ed., *Rule of Saint Benedict 1980* (Collegeville, MN: Liturgical Press, 1981).

Chapter 1

1. Olivier Clément, *The Roots of Christian Mysticism: Text and Commentary* (New York: New City Press, 1995), 318.

2. J.B. Lightfoot, trans., "The Letter of the Smyrnaeans or the Martyrdom of Polycarp," *Early Christian Writings*, http://www.earlychristianwritings.com/text/martyrdompolycarp-lightfoot.html.

3. One of the best sources is www.osb.org, where you will find the complete text of the Rule in English in Leonard Boyle's translation, http://www.osb.org/rb/text/toc.html; and the daily reading of the Rule that Benedictines around the world use, http://www.osb.org/rb/show.asp?mode=today.

4. Timothy Fry, ed., *Rule of Saint Benedict 1980* (Collegeville, MN: Liturgical Press, 1981).

5. An excellent guide to *lectio* is Michael Casey, *Sacred Reading: The Ancient Art of Lectio Divina* (Liguori, MO: Liguori/Triumph, 1996).

6. Ancient Christian Commentary on Scripture series, ed. Thomas C. Oden (Downers Grove, IL: InterVarsity Press).

Chapter 2

1. Tony Hillerman, *The Ghostway* (New York: HarperCollins, 1984), 98.

2. Melissa Musick Nussbaum, "The Secret to how we spend our last days," *National Catholic Reporter*, October 23, 2013, http://ncronline.org/blogs/my-table-spread/secret-how-we-spend-our-last-days.

3. Nina Bernstein, "Fighting to Honor a Father's Last Wish: To Die at Home," *The New York Times*, September 25, 2014, http://www.nytimes.com/2014/09/26/nyregion/family-fights-health-care-system-for-simple-request-to-die-at-home.html?_r=0.

4. Andrew Weil, *Healthy Aging: A Lifelong Guide to Your Physical and Spiritual Well-Being* (New York: Alfred A. Knopf, 2005), 50.

5. Ibid., 52.

6. Gerd Gigerenzer et al., "Helping Doctors and Patients Make Sense of Health Statistics," *Psychological Science in the Public Interest* 8, no. 2 (2008), http://web.mit.edu/5.95/readings/gigerenzer.pdf.

7. C. S. Lewis, *The Four Loves* (New York: HarperCollins, 1960), 122–23.

8. Lewis, *The Screwtape Letters* (London: Collins Fontana Books, 1966), 108.

9. Olivier Clément, *The Roots of Christian Mysticism: Text and Commentary* (New York: New City Press, 1995), 82.

10. David Snowdon, *Aging with Grace: What the Nun Study Teaches Us About Leading Longer, Healthier, and More Meaningful Lives* (New York: Bantam Books, 2001), 203.

11. Ibid., 194, 202–3.

12. Dan Buettner, *The Blue Zones: Lessons for Living Longer from the People Who've Lived the Longest* (Washington, DC: National Geographic Society, 2008), 231–62.

13. Dante, *Purgatory*, trans. Dorothy L. Sayers (London: Penguin, 1955), 209.

14. Dorothy L. Sayers, *Creed or Chaos?* (London: Methuen, 1947), 84–85.

15. Wendy Wasserstein, *Sloth: The Seven Deadly Sins*, New York Public Library Lectures in the Humanities (New York: Oxford University Press, 2005), ProQuest ebrary, Web 105–6.

16. James A. Levine, "What Are the Risks of Sitting Too Much?," MayoClinic.org, http://www.mayoclinic.org/healthy-living/adult-health/expert-answers/sitting/faq-20058005.

17. Snowdon, *Aging with Grace*, 38.

18. Austin Flannery, ed., *Vatican Council II: Constitutions, Decrees, Declarations; The Basic Sixteen Documents* (Collegeville, MN: Liturgical Press, 2014).

19. Virgil Elizondo, "Introduction: Pilgrimage: An Enduring Ritual of Humanity," *Concilium* 1996/4, http://www.bijbel.net/concilium/?b=25993.

20. Helen Waddell, trans., *The Desert Fathers* (New York: Henry Hold, 1936), 139.

Chapter 3

1. "The Ugly Truth About Food Waste in America," *Talk of the Nation*, November 23, 2012, http://www.npr.org/2012/11/23/165774988/npr-the-ugly-truth-about-food-waste-in-america.

2. *Catechesis* (June 5, 2013), *Insegnamenti* 1/1 (2013): 280. See also Basil the Great, *Ascetical Works*, trans. M. Monica Wagner (Washington, DC: Catholic University of America Press, 1950), 280.

3. Cyril of Alexandria, Meditation on the Mystical Supper 10, quoted in Joel C. Elowsky, ed., *Ancient Christian Commentary on Scripture: John 1–10* (Downers Grove, IL: InterVarsity Press, 2006), 241.

4. Graham Ward, *Christ and Culture* (Oxford: Blackwell, 2005), 105.

5. Irenaeus of Lyons, *Against Heresies*, quoted in Olivier Clément, *The Roots of Christian Mysticism: Text and Commentary* (New York: New City Press, 1995), 89.

6. Angel F. Méndez-Montoya, *The Theology of Food: Eating and the Eucharist* (Chichester: Wiley-Blackwell, 2012), 148.

7. Harold S. Kushner, *To Life! A Celebration of Jewish Being and Thinking* (Boston: Little, Brown, 1993), 56.

8. Thomas P. Ryan, *The Sacred Art of Fasting: Preparing to Practice* (Woodstock, VT: Skylight Paths, 2005), 15.

9. Ryan, *Art of Fasting*, 27, quoting Aliza Bulow, "Connecting through Fasting," Aish.com, http://www.aish.com/h/9av/oal /Connecting_Through_Fasting.html.

10. Robert J. Karris, *Eating Your Way through Luke's Gospel* (Collegeville, MN: Liturgical Press, 2006), 14, 97–98.

11. Clément, *The Roots of Christian Mysticism*, 131.

12. James David O'Neill, "The Black Fast," *The Catholic Encyclopedia*, vol. 2 (New York: Robert Appleton, 1907), http://www .newadvent.org/cathen/02590c.htm.

13. Joseph F. Wimmer, *Fasting in the New Testament: A Study in Biblical Theology* (Mahwah, NJ: Paulist Press, 1982), 52.

14. Eamon Duffy, "To Fast Again," *First Things* (March 2005): 4–5.

15. Chaucer, *The Canterbury Tales*, trans. Ronald L. Ecker and Eugene J. Crook (Hodge & Braddock, 1993), line 830, http://english .fsu.edu/canterbury/parson.html.

16. Dan Charles, "Our Favorite Banana May Be Doomed; Can New Varieties Replace It?," *All Things Considered*, January 11, 2016, http://www.npr.org/sections/thesalt/2016/01/11/462375558 /our-favorite-banana-may-be-doomed-can-new-varieties-replace-it.

17. Michael Pollan, *In Defense of Food: An Eater's Manifesto* (New York: Penguin, 2008), 90.

18. "How Western Diets Are Making The World Sick," *Fresh Air*, March 24, 2011, http://www.npr.org/2011/03/24/132745785 /how-western-diets-are-making-the-world-sick.

19. Pollan, *In Defense of Food*, 87.

20. Chaucer, *The Canterbury Tales*, line 835.

21. Gregory Baum, "Structures of Sin," in *The Logic of Solidarity: Commentaries on Pope John Paul II's Encyclical "On Social Concern,"* ed. Gregory Baum and Robert Ellsberg, 112 (Maryknoll, NY: Orbis Books, 1989).

22. Doris Janzen Longacre, *More-with-Less Cookbook*, updated ed. (Harrisonburg, VA: Herald Press, 2011).

23. Barbara Kingsolver, *Animal, Vegetable, Miracle: A Year of Food Life* (New York: Harper, 2007).

24. Daniel J. DeNoon, "7 Rules for Eating," March 23, 2009, http://www.webmd.com/food-recipes/20090323/7-rules-for-eating. See also Michael Pollan, *Food Rules: An Eater's Manual* (New York: Penguin, 2009).

25. The Resiliency Institute, "Growing Food Security," http://www.theresiliencyinstitute.net/programs/growing-food-security/.

26. Méndez-Montoya, *Theology of Food*, 26.

Chapter 4

1. Kelly McGonigal, *The Upside of Stress: Why Stress is Good for You and How to Get Good at It* (New York: Penguin, 2015), 66.

2. Ibid., 84.

3. Francis, *Laudato Sì* (On Care for Our Common Home) 22, http://w2.vatican.va/content/francesco/en/encyclicals/documents/papa-francesco_20150524_enciclica-laudato-si.html.

4. McGonigal, *Upside of Stress*, 70.

5. This website has a helpful guide: http://www.ignatianspirituality.com/ignatian-prayer/the-what-how-why-of-prayer/review-prayer-by-keeping-a-journal.

6. Francis, *Amoris Laetitia* 33, post-synodal apostolic exhortation on love in the family, March 19, 2016, http://w2.vatican.va/content/francesco/en/apost_exhortations/documents/papa-francesco_esortazione-ap_20160319_amoris-laetitia.html.

7. See Dorothy L. Sayers, *The Mind of the Maker* (New York: HarperCollins, 1987). For a fuller discussion of Sayers's analogy and its implications for work, see Christine M. Fletcher, *The Artist and the Trinity* (Eugene, OR: Pickwick Press, 2011).

8. Sayers, *Mind of the Maker*, 209–10.

9. Peter Korn, *Why We Make Things and Why It Matters: The Education of a Craftsman* (Boston, MA: David R. Godine, 2013), 10, 13.

10. Sayers, "Why Work?," in *Creed or Chaos?* (London: Methuen, 1947), 193.

11. Mihaly Csikszentmihalyi, *Creativity: Flow and the Psychology of Discovery and Invention* (New York: HarperPerennial, 1996), 110–13.

12. Alasdair MacIntyre, *After Virtue* (Notre Dame, IN: University of Notre Dame Press, 1984), 187.

13. Oliver Sacks, "Sabbath," *The New York Times*, Opinion (August 14, 2015).

Chapter 5

1. Pew Research Center, *Religious Landscape Study*, 2014, http://www.pewforum.org/religious-landscape-study/.

2. Pew Research Center, "Leaving, Joining and Staying in the Catholic Church," *U.S. Catholics Open to Non-Traditional Families*, September 2, 2015, http://www.pewforum.org/2015/09/02/u-s-catholics-open-to-non-traditional-families/.

3. See *Evangelii Nuntiandi*, December 8, 1975, http://w2.vatican.va/content/paul-vi/en/apost_exhortations/documents/hf_p-vi_exh_19751208_evangelii-nuntiandi.html.

4. John Paul II, homily, apostolic pilgrimage to Poland, June 9, 1979, http://w2.vatican.va/content/john-paul-ii/en/homilies/1979/documents/hf_jp-ii_hom_19790609_polonia-mogila-nowa-huta.html.

5. John Paul II, *Redemptoris Missio*, December 7, 1990, http://w2.vatican.va/content/john-paul-ii/en/encyclicals/documents/hf_jp-ii_enc_07121990_redemptoris-missio.html.

6. United States Conference of Catholic Bishops, The New Evangelization: Disciples on Mission in the World. Available at http://www.usccb.org/beliefs-and-teachings/how-we-teach/new-evangelization/.

7. Sherry A. Weddell, *Forming Intentional Disciples: The Path to Knowing and Following Jesus* (Huntington, IN: Our Sunday Visitor, 2012).

8. Weddell adapted the thresholds from Don Everts and Doug Schaupp, *I Once Was Lost: What Postmodern Skeptics Taught Us About Their Path to Jesus* (Downers Grove, IL: InterVarsity Press, 2008).

9. Charles de Foucauld, http://www.vatican.va/news_services/liturgy/saints/ns_lit_doc_20051113_de-foucauld_en.html.

10. "Prayer of Abandonment—Charles de Foucauld," Crossroads Initiative, https://www.crossroadsinitiative.com/media/articles/prayer-of-abandonment-charles-de-foucauld/.

Chapter 6

1. Augustine of Hippo, Sermon 346, I (*PL* 38.1522).

2. Olivier Clément, *The Roots of Christian Mysticism: Text and Commentary* (New York: New City Press, 1995), 316.

3. Sherwin B. Nuland, *How We Die: Reflections on Life's Final Chapter* (New York: Vintage Books, 1995), 248.

4. John Swinton and Richard Payne, eds., *Living Well and Dying Faithfully: Christian Practices for End-of-Life Care* (Grand Rapids, MI: Eerdmans, 2009), xv.

5. Atul Gawande, *Being Mortal: Medicine and What Matters in the End* (New York: Metropolitan Books, 2014), 171–72.

6. Ira Byock, *Dying Well: Peace and Possibilities at the End of Life* (New York: Riverhead Books, 1997), 243.

7. Charles G. Sasser, "Foreword," in *Living at the End of Life: A Hospice Nurse Addresses the Most Common Questions*, Karen Whitley Bell, ix (New York: Sterling Ethos, 2010).

8. Maggie Callanan and Patricia Kelley, *Final Gifts: Understanding the Special Awareness, Needs, and Communications of the Dying* (New York: Poseidon Press, 1992), xvi.

9. Ibid.

10. Byock, *Dying Well*, 243.

11. Ezekiel Emanuel, "Why I Hope to Die at 75," *The Atlantic*, October 2014, http://www.theatlantic.com/magazine/archive/2014/10/why-i-hope-to-die-at-75/379329/.

12. Byock, *Dying Well*, 247.

13. Gawande, *Being Mortal*, 161.

14. Ibid., 178.

15. Ibid.

16. Ibid.

17. Pius XII, "Prolongation of Life," *The Pope Speaks* 4 (1958): 395–96.

18. Pius XII, "Cancer, a Medical and Social Problem," quoted in Richard C. Sparks, *To Treat or Not to Treat: Bioethics and the Handicapped Newborn* (Mahwah, NJ: Paulist Press, 1988), 92.

19. Basil, *Ascetical Works*, trans. M. Monica Wagner (Washington, DC: Catholic University of America Press, 1962), 331.

20. John Paul II, *Evangelium Vitae* 15, http://w2.vatican.va /content/john-paul-ii/en/encyclicals/documents/hf_jp-ii_enc _25031995_evangelium-vitae.html.

21. *Catechism of the Catholic Church*, 2nd ed. (United States Catholic Conference—Libreria Editrice Vaticana, 1997), 399.

22. Benedict XVI, *Spe Salvi* 42, November 30, 2007, http:// w2.vatican.va/content/benedict-xvi/en/encyclicals/documents/hf _ben-xvi_enc_20071130_spe-salvi.html.

Chapter 7

1. Anon., *Ars Bene Moriendi*, ed. Benjamin Pifteau (Paris: Delarue, n.d. [1880/1889?]), in *Medieval Popular Religion, 1000–1500: A Reader*, 2nd ed., trans. John Shinners, 548 (Peterborough, Ontario: Broadview Press, 2006).

2. Frances M. M. Comper, *The Book of the Craft of Dying and Other Early English Tracts Concerning Death* (London: Longmans, Green, 1917), 24–26.

3. George McCauley, *Sacraments for Secular Man* (Danville, NJ: Dimension Books, 1969), 73.

4. Comper, *Craft of Dying*, 16.

5. Ibid., 18.

6. Ibid., 19.

7. Ibid., 27.

8. Ibid., 73–74.

9. Nortin Hadler, *Rethinking Aging: Growing Old and Living Well in an Overtreated Society* (Chapel Hill, NC: University of North Carolina Press, 2011), 196.